The Siege of Savannah

A Da Capo Press Reprint Series

THE ERA OF THE AMERICAN REVOLUTION

GENERAL EDITOR: LEONARD W. LEVY

Claremont Graduate School

The Siege of Savannah

By The Combined American and French Forces
Under the Command of Gen. Lincoln
and the Count D'Estaing
In the Autumn of 1779.

Edited by
Franklin Benjamin Hough

DA CAPO PRESS • NEW YORK • 1974

Library of Congress Cataloging in Publication Data

Hough, Franklin Benjamin, 1822-1885, ed.
    The siege of Savannah.

    (The Era of the American Revolution)
    Reprint of the 1866 ed. published by J. Munsell, Albany.
    1. Savannah, Ga.--Siege, 1779. I. Title.
E241.S26H8 1974   975.8'724   77-165683
ISBN 0-306-70619-9

This Da Capo Press edition of *The Siege of Savannah is an unabridged*
republication of the first edition published in Albany, New York in 1866.
It is reprinted from a copy in the collections of The Free Library of Philadelphia.

Published by Da Capo Press, Inc.
A Subsidiary of Plenum Publishing Corporation
227 West 17th Street, New York, N.Y. 10011

Thomas Pinckney

THE

Siege of Savannah,

BY THE

˙COMBINED AMERICAN AND FRENCH FORCES,

UNDER THE COMMAND OF

GEN. LINCOLN, AND THE COUNT D'ESTAING,

IN THE

Autumn of 1779.

ALBANY
J. MUNSELL, 82 STATE STREET
1866

PREFACE.

HE unfortunate Issue of the Enterprise undertaken in 1779, to recover Possession of the Capital of Georgia, has left a gloomy Page in our Revolutionary History, not only from its Failure as a military Movement, but from the melancholy Casualty which deprived our Army of one of its most talented Leaders, the Polish General Count Pulaski.

The Depression of the Patriots of the Revolution by these Reverses, was destined to be still further increased by the subsequent Success of the British Arms in the Southern Colonies, while it afforded Cause of Exultation among the Loyalists, who confidently predicted the speedy and effectual Reftoration of the Royal Authority throughout the revolted Colonies.

The Columns of the *Royal Gazette* bear Witnefs to the Strength of this Hope, while they at the fame Time exhibit the Feeling of Bitternefs which they cherifhed towards thofe who had begun the War, and in which the Infurgents had already achieved Succefs on many Occafions.

The following Pages prefent the Accounts that were publifhed in Mr. Rivington's Paper, upon the Subject of the unfuccefsful Attempt of the combined American and French Forces to capture the City of Savannah, in the Months of September and October, 1779.

According to the Plan propofed for this Series, we have briefly ftated the Circum-ftances which preceded and attended the Event, before prefenting the Documents that embrace the Details; and have placed in the Appendix, fuch other Statements and Papers, as would more fully prefent the Subject in all its Bearings, and under every Point of View.

INTRODUCTION.

THE Manifeſtations of Sympathy with the Revolution in the Colony of Georgia, although perhaps not leſs earneſt, was leſs aggreſſive than in the North, and did not attract the Notice of the Britiſh Adminiſtration as requiring particular Effort on their Part in the earlier Years of the War. Although the Patriots of that Section entered into the Meaſures aiming at a Reform in Government with great Zeal, it was doubtleſs believed that when once the Armies in the North were vanquiſhed, the whole Country would acquieſce in the Neceſſity of Obedience to the Britiſh Rule, without the Trouble of ſending coſtly Armies and Navies to receive the Submiſſion of the late Inſurgents.

B

The Number of Sympathizers with the British Cause, was relatively much larger than in the northern Colonies, and in Proportion as this Cause prevailed, large Numbers of the Colonists lent their willing Aid in its Support, or paſſively yielded their Acquiefcence to its Terms.

There were however, many earneſt and vigorous Advocates of the Revolution, efpecially in the Upper Country, and the partizan Warfare which they continued to maintain long after the Cities on the Coaſt had been apparently fettled as permanent Dependencies of the Crown, furnifhes fome of the moſt brilliant Paſſages in our Revolutionary Hiſtory. The Conteſt became in fome Parts a War of Extermination, and it appeared as if one Party muſt be entirely rooted out, before the other could live in Peace.

The Events of the War having fhown that the Prefence of a Britifh Army was neceſſary to the Maintenance of the Royal Caufe, and probably in the Expectation that with this Encouragement, the loyal Portions of the Population, would venture to Rally in Force around the Britifh Standard, an Expedition was fitted out from New York towards the Clofe of 1779, to eftablifh themfelves at Savannah.

The American Force at that Place, then confifted of between fix and feven hundred Continentals, and a few hundred Militia under the Command of Major General Robert Howe.

The official Report of the Britifh Officer who led this Expedition is embraced in the following Letter addreffed to Lord George Germain, dated "Savannah, January 16, 1779:"

"In confequence of Orders from Sir Henry Clinton, to proceed to Georgia with his Majefty's 71ft Regiment of Foot, two Battalions of Heffians, four Battalions of Provincials, and a Detachment of the Royal Artillery, Colonel Archibald Campbell embarked at Sandy Hook on the 27th November, 1778, and arrived off the Ifland of

Tybee on the 23d December, escorted by a
Squadron under the Command of Commodore Parker. On the 24th, the greatest
Part of the Transports got over the Bar and
anchored in Savannah River. On the 27th,
the Balance of Commodore Parker's Fleet
joined him. During the Time occupied in
bringing the last Division of the Fleet over
the Bar, from the Provincial Battalions,
were formed two Corps of Light Infantry,
the one to be attached to Sir James Baird's
light Company of the 71st Highlanders,
the other to Captain Cameron's Company
of the same Regiment. Having no Intelligence that could be depended upon with
respect to the military Force of Georgia, or
the Dispositions formed for its Defence, Sir
James Baird's Highland Company of Light
Infantry, in two Flat-boats, with Lieutenant Clarke, of the Navy, was dispatched in
the Night of the 25th, to seize any of the
Inhabitants they might find on the Banks
of Wilmington River. Two Men were
taken, from whom the Enemy derived In-

formation which they confidered Satisfactory, and induced them to refolve to land the Troops the next Evening at the Plantation of Mr. Gerredeaux, twelve Miles further up the River, and two Miles from the Town of Savannah. The Vigilant Man-of-war, with the Comet Galley, the Keppel armed Brig, and the Greenwich armed Sloop, followed by the Tranfports in three Divifions, in the Order eftablifhed for a Defcent, proceeded up the River with the Tide, at Noon. About four o'clock in the Evening the Vigilant opened the Reach to Gerredeaux's Plantation, and was cannonaded by two American Galleys.

" The Tide and Evening being too far fpent, and many of the Tranfports having been grounded at the Diftance of five or fix Miles below Gerredeaux's Plantation, the Defcent was delayed until next Morning. The firft Divifion of Troops, confifting of all the Light Infantry of the Army, the New York Volunteers, and the firft Battalion of the 71ft, under the Command of

Lieutenant-Colonel Maitland, were landed
at Break of Day on the River Dam in front
of Gerredeaux's, from whence a narrow
Caufeway of fix hundred Yards in Length,
with a Ditch on each Side, led through a
Swamp directly for Gerredeaux's Houfe,
which ftood upon a Bluff about thirty Feet
high. The Light Infantry, under Captain
Cameron, having firft reached the Shore,
were formed, and led brifkly forward to the
Bluff, where a Body of fifty Americans were
pofted, and from whom they received a
fmart Fire of Mufketry; but the Enemy
rufhed forward and drove them into the
Woods, and fecured a Landing for the Reft
of the Army. Captain Cameron and two
Highlanders were killed, and five Highlanders wounded. The Army of Major-
General Howe was drawn up about Half a
Mile Eaft of the City of Savannah, with
feveral Pieces of Cannon in their Front.
The firft Divifion of Troops, together with
one Company of the fecond Battalion of
the 71ft, the firft Battalion of Delancey's,

the Wellworth, and a Part of the Wiffenbach Regiment of Heffians being landed,
Colonel Campbell went in Purfuit of the
Americans, leaving a confiderable Force to
cover the Landing-place. On the Troops
reaching the Road leading to Savannah, the
Divifion of the Wiffenbach Regiment was
pofted on the Crofs-roads, to fecure the Rear
of the Army; a thick Swamp covered the
Left of the Line of March, and the Light
Infantry, with the Flankers of each Corps,
effectually covered the cultivated Plantations
on the Right. The Troops reached the
open Country, near Tattnall's Plantation,
before three o'Clock in the Afternoon, and
halted on the Road about two hundred
Paces fhort of the Gate leading to Governor
Wright's Plantation.

" The American Army were drawn up
acrofs the Road, at the Diftance of eight
hundred Yards from this Gateway. One-
half, confifting of Thompfon's and Huger's
Regiments of Carolina Troops, were formed

under Col. Huger, with their Left oblique to the Road leading to Savannah, their Right to a wooded Swamp covered by the Houſes of Tatnall's Plantation, in which ſome Riflemen had been placed. The other Half of the American Army, confiſting of Part of the firſt, ſecond, third, and fourth Battalions of the Georgia Brigade, was formed under Colonel Elbert, with their Right to the Road, and their Left to the Rice Swamps of Governor Wright's Plantation, with the Fort of Savannah Bluff behind their left Wing, in the Style of a ſecond Flank; the Town of Savannah, round which were the Remains of an old Line of Intrenchment, covered their Rear. One Piece of Cannon was planted on the Right of their Line, about one hundred Paces in Front of the Traverſe. At a Spot between two Swamps a Trench was cut acroſs the Road; and about one hundred Yards in Front of this Trench a marſhy Rivulet run almoſt parallel the whole Extent of their Front; the Bridge of which was burnt down, to interrupt the Paſſage and retard the Progreſs of the Engliſh.

Colonel Campbell diſcovered, from the Movements of the Americans, that they expeＣted an Attack upon their Left, and he was deſirous of confirming that ExpeＣtation. Having fallen in with a Negro named Quamino Dolly, Colonel Campbell induced him, by a ſmall Reward, to conduＣt the Troops, by a private Path through the Swamp, upon the Right of the Americans. Colonel Campbell ordered the firſt Battalion of the 71ſt to form on his Right of the Road, and move up to the Rear of the Light Infantry, whilſt he drew off that Corps to the Right, as if he meant to extend his Front to that Quarter, where a Fall of Ground favoured the Concealment of this Manœuvre. Sir James Baird had Orders to convey the Light Infantry to the hollow Ground quite to the Rear, and penetrate the Swamp upon the Enemy's Left, with a

C

View to get round, by the new Barracks,
into the Rear of the Enemy's right Flank.
The New York Volunteers, under Colonel
Tumbull, were ordered to fupport him.
During the Courfe of this Movement, the
Enemy's Artillery were formed in a Field
on their Left of the Road, concealed from
the Americans by a Swell of Ground in
Front, to which Colonel Campbell meant
to run them up for Action, when the Signal
was made to engage, and from whence he
could either bear advantageoufly upon the
Right of the American Line as it was then
formed, or cannonade any Body of Troops
in Flank which they might detach into the
Wood to retard the Progrefs of the Light
Infantry. Campbell then commenced the
Attack, and the American Line was broken.
About one hundred of the Georgia Militia,
under the Command of Colonel George
Walton, pofted at the new Barracks with
fome Pieces of Cannon, were attacked by
Sir James Baird, and after fighting bravely,
were compelled to retreat. The General

(Howe) ordered a general Retreat, which was made in great Confufion."

In the Capture of Savannah, the Americans loft about one hundred killed on the Field, or drowned in endeavoring to retreat, and thirty-eight Officers and four hundred and fifteen Privates were captured. All their Cannon, Munitions and Provifions fell into the Enemy's Hands, with but the moderate Lofs on their Part of feven killed and nineteen wounded. No Blame was, under the Circumftances, attached to General Howe, who was fubfequently honorably acquitted by a Court of Inquiry.[1]

A conciliatory Policy was adopted by the Victors, which attracted Multitudes of the Inhabitants to the Royal Caufe. A Series of fuccefsful Movements againft Sunbury, Augufta and other Points, feemed to decide the future Deftinies of this Colony, and

---

[1] The Loffes of the Americans befides in Men, were, one Stand of Colours, forty-eight Cannon, twenty-three Mortars, ninety-four Barrels of Powder, and the Fort with all its Stores. Savannah was then the Capital of Georgia.

called the Attention of Congreſs to the Neceſſity of making a deciſive Effort to regain their Loſſes in the Southern Department.

Charleſton was at this Time an important Poſt ſtill in the Hands of the Americans, but was dependent upon the civil Authorities for its Supplies, and Embarraſſments exiſted in the local Adminiſtration which threatened the moſt ſerious Conſequences.

In the preceding September, a Change had been ordered in the Command of the Southern Department, by which General Benjamin Lincoln of Maſſachuſetts, was aſſigned to that Poſt, and General Howe was directed to report to General Waſhington. Under this Arrangement Gen. Lincoln had proceeded to Charleſton, from whence, upon learning of the Entrance of the Britiſh Fleet into the Savannah River, he marched to the Relief of Gen. Howe, but upon arriving at a Point on the north Side of the River he learned of the Diſaſter which had happened below, and was foon joined by the Remnant of the defeated Army.

The Savannah River now remained for fome Time the dividing Line between the two Forces. The whole of Georgia was confidered fo far under Britifh Authority, that a civil Government was eftablifhed, and executive and judicial Officers appointed.

The Frontiers were however not allowed to remain quiet, and the early Months of 1779 were fpent in alternate aggreffive and defenfive Movements by General Lincoln and General Prevoft,[1] in the Courfe of which, the former undertook to eftablifh himfelf at Augufta, while the latter attacked Charlefton from the land Side, but without Succefs. After a Series of Operations upon the Iflands on the Coaft the Britifh Army returned to Savannah and St. Auguftine,

[1] Major General Auguftine Prevoft was then in Command. His Rank dated from May 25, 1772. He failed for England in the Brig *Three Friends*, foon after the Siege of Savannah was raifed. He was a Native of Switzerland, and died in 1786. His Son George was Governor in Canada in the War of 1812–15.

after eftablifhing a Poft on the Ifland con-
tiguous to Port Royal and St. Helena, and
at various Points in the Interior, while
General Lincoln with about eight hundred
Men retired to Sheldon, near Beaufort, to
prepare for the next Campaign, which it
was fuppofed would open in October.

The French, then at War with the Englifh, had at this Time a large Fleet in the
Weft Indies. The Britifh Forces had captured St. Lucia, and the French had reduced St. Vincents and Grenada, and at
about the Time when the latter Event occurred, the Count d'Eftaing, who commanded the French Fleet, received fuch
large Reinforcements as to give him for the
Time being a decided naval Superiority.

A Reprefentation was accordingly made
to the Count d'Eftaing, by Governor Rutledge of South Carolina and General Lincoln, in Concert with M. Plombard, French
Conful at Charlefton, which induced him
to undertake with the Continental Forces
under General Lincoln, a combined Attack

upon their common Enemy, the Englifh, at Savannah.

The Propofition being favorably received, the Count, in Conformity to his Inftructions to aid the Americans whenever a fair Opportunity fhould offer, prepared to undertake the Enterprife. He accordingly left Cape François, with twenty-two Ships of the Line and eleven Frigates, having on board fix thoufand land Troops and appeared at the Mouth of the Savannah River, before the Englifh had got Intelligence of the Plan, and at a Time when they were leaft expecting a hoftile Vifit.

The firft Intimation of the Approach of the French Fleet was received by General Prevoft on the third of September. He haftened to call in the Forces under Colonel Maitland at Port Royal, and feveral Detachments in the Interior for the Defence of the Capital.

General Lincoln upon being notified of thefe Movements, marched to coöperate with the Forces under his Command, but

his Route was greatly delayed by the De-
ſtruction of Bridges and the Want of Tranſ-
portation, and he did not effect a Junction
until the ſixteenth.

The Count d'Eſtaing had before this, demanded a Surrender of the Town, but had
unwiſely allowed the Correſpondence which
enſued to delay his own Operations, while
this Interval was actively improved by General Prevoſt in preparing for a vigorous
Defence. One can ſcarcely read this Correſpondence without being convinced, that
it was protracted by the Britiſh as long as
poſſible to await the Arrival of their Reinforcements. Although the French held the
main Channel of the River, there were ſtill
ſeveral Routes behind the Iſlands which
they could not blockade. The Engliſh on
their Part, ſunk Veſſels in the River, to
hinder the Paſſage of the French Fleet, and
called into Service all the Labor that could
be reached, to erect Fortifications before
the Town.

The Siege began on the 23d of September and on the 1ft of October he had advanced within three hundred Yards of the Britifh Works, Batteries were planted, and a heavy Cannonade opened upon the Britifh Works and the Town. The Profecution of the Siege, by regular Approaches, was a Work of Time, and the Seafon was getting late and dangerous for the Fleet upon an infecure Coaft and at a Period when Tempefts become frequent and deftructive.

It was therefore refolved to attempt to carry the Place by Affault. On the 9th of October an Attack was made along a hollow Way on the Left of the allied Army which covered the Advance, to within fifty Yards of the main Works, while Feints were made by the Militia at other Points. The Affault was made in three Columns by about three thoufand five hundred French and one thoufand Americans, including Continentals and Charlefton Militia.

These Columns were met by a more

D

vigorous Refiftance than was expected, yet
they preffed forward with Ardor, paffed
through the Abatis and Ditch and mounted
the Parapet, where both French and Americans, planted their Standards, but they were
finally compelled to Retreat with heavy
Lofs.   The Count Pulafki, while charging
at the Head of about two hundred Horfe,
in the Rear, received a fevere Wound of
which he died a few Days after.   The
Count d'Eftaing and Major General De
Montange were alfo wounded.

  After this Repulfe, the Count d'Eftaing
refolved to raife the Siege.   The Remon-
ftrances of General Lincoln proved unavail-
ing, and the Removal of the heavy Ordnance and Stores was commenced.   The
American Army recroffed the Savannah at
Zubly's Ferry, and took Poft again in South
Carolina, while the French Fleet paffed
out of the River and difappeared from the
Coaft.

  A violent Gale difperfed this Fleet, fo
that though the Count had directed feven

Sail to repair to the Chefapeake, but one
Veffel was able to execute the Order. A
Portion returned to the Weft Indies and
the Reft to France.

The City of Savannah had at this Time
about four hundred and thirty Houfes, and
it fuffered confiderably from the Siege.
The Strength of the Englifh Garrifon was
eftimated at fomewhat lefs than three thoufand Men, and the Succefs with which they
held the Place reflected great Credit upon
their Valor and Spirit, while the Refult
depreffed the Spirits of the American Army
in a correfponding Degree. The high
Expectations of Victory which had brought
the Militia into the Field, were fuddenly
checked, and the Affairs of the Southern
States wore a more gloomy Afpect than at
any former Period.[1]

Colonel Maitland whofe opportune Arrival probably decided the Fate of Savannah
upon this Occafion, fhared the Labors and

[1] *Marfhall's Wafhington,* iv, 104.

Perils of the Siege, but foon after fickened and died of a Fever.

The Englifh were not again difturbed in their Occupation of Savannah until they voluntarily withdrew on the 11th of July, 1782, leaving the Town in Poffeffion to the American Authorities, and the Colony to its future Deftiny as one of the States of the new Republic.

JOURNAL

OF THE

SIEGE OF SAVANNAH.

[From Rivington's Royal Gazette, No. 334, Dec. 11, 1779.]

By the Brig Elphingſton, Capt. Kennedy, who arrived here this Day, in fourteen Days from Georgia, we have received the following Advices :

SAVANNAH, November 18.

ON Friday, the third of September laſt, ſeveral large Ships were ſeen off our Bar, and a Boat being ſent out by Captain Brown, of his Majeſty's Ship *Roſe*,[1] with a Lieutenant on Board, they were plainly diſcovered to be French.

---

[1] This Veſſel was ſunk in the Channel, September 20th, to obſtruct the River againſt the Approach of the French Fleet.

Monday Evening the 6th, a Sloop called the *General Mathews*, came up to Town. On the Thurſday before, ſhe was taken to the northward of the Bar, by a French 74 Ship. They took all the People out of her, except one Man, and put five Frenchmen in their Room. In the Gale of Wind that Night, ſhe parted from the Man-of-war, and on Saturday Morning, arriving off Tybee, the Engliſhman told the Frenchmen that it was the Entrance to Charleſtown, and by that Means ſoon brought the Sloop to Anchor in the Mouth of the River. After the Arrival of this Veſſel, it was ſaid, that the Fleet conſiſted of the *Magnifique*, of 74, and *Sphinx*, of 64 Guns, (Part of a Reinforcement of four Line-of-battle Ships lately ſent from France to join Count d'-Eſtaing in the Weſt Indies), two Frigates, a Schooner, and a Cutter, all from Cape François, bound to Boſton for Maſts and Spars.

On Tueſday the 7th, a Number of Veſ-ſels appeared off Tybee Bar, but went off

again, and next Day, about 51 were reck-
oned off Waſſaw, 25 of which were ſaid to
be Ships of the Line.

Thurſday Morning the 9th, they were
all off Tybee again, and ſome of them fired
at Captain McDonough's Packetboat from
St. Auguſtine, attempting to get in, which
fell into their Hands. That Evening, four
Frigates got over the Bar, and came to an
anchor at Tybee, and in the Night, or early
next Morning, landed a Number of Men
on the Iſland. His Majeſty's Ship *Savannah, Comet* Galley and ſome other Veſſels,
were ordered up the River to ſtrengthen
the Garriſon on the French Veſſels getting
over the Bar.

The French who had landed reëmbarked
on Friday the 10th, and. all the Fleet,
except the Frigates at Anchor at Tybee,
ſteered for the Southward. Next Day they
appeared again off the Bar.

It ſeemed now evident, that they intended a ſerious Attack on this Place. We had

for fome Time been repairing the four old Redoubts, and making fome additional Works, having been threatened with an Attack from the Rebels. But now the greateft and moft extraordinary Exertions were made by Captain Moncrief,[1] Chief Engineer, and which he continued during the whole Siege with unremitting Ardor. Betwixt two and three hundred Negroes were ordered in by the Governor[2] and Council, immediately fet to Work, and thirteen good Redoubts were foon erected round the Town, and 15 Gun Batteries containing about 76 Pieces of Cannon, 18, 9 and 6 Pounders, were raifed between the Redoubts. Thefe Batteries were manned by the Sailors of the Ships of War, Tranf-ports and Merchantmen, in the River, be-fides which, there were feveral Four-pound-

[1] Capt. George Moncrieffe of the 81ft Regiment.   His Rank dated December 23, 1777.

[2] Sir James Wright, Baronet, was at this Time Governor of Georgia.

ers, properly placed without the Batteries, and five Field Pieces.

On Sunday Night the 11th, the French began to land their Troops at Bewlie, about 14 Miles from Town.

Thurſday the 16th, in the Forenoon, a Letter was ſent into Camp by Count d'Eſ-taing, the French General, DEMANDING A SURRENDER OF THE TOWN TO THE FRENCH KING.[1] He was then within three Miles of this Place. He boaſt-ed in his Letter, of his formidable Arma-ment by Sea and Land; the great Feats he had performed with it in the Weſt Indies, and mentioned how much Lord McCartney had ſuffered by not capitulating at Grenada, and that it was in vain to think of reſiſting his Force, warned General Prevoſt, againſt the Conſequences attending the Place being taken by Storm, and hinted that he would be anſwerable for the Lives of the People that might be Loſt, &c. The Anſwer re-

[1] This Correſpondence is given on a ſubſequent Page.

E

turned to this Letter by General Prevoſt,
was to the following Purport: That he
hoped the Count had a better Opinion of
him, and the Britiſh Army he had the
Honor to Command, than to expeᵈ they
would ſurrender the Town, &c. on a general Summons, without knowing on what
ſpecific Terms or Conditions: That if he
had any Terms to offer, he deſired they
might be made known; and mentioned his
having communicated the Contents of his
Letter to the civil Governor.

To this the Count replied, that it was the
Part of the Beſieged, and not the Beſiegers,
to propoſe Terms: Upon which it was ſig-
nified to him, that it was a Matter of great
Conſequence, and that there were many
different Intereſts to be adjuſted and ſettled,
and therefore it was deſired, that twenty-
four Hours might be allowed to conſider it.
The Count accordingly agreed to wait till
the firing of the Evening Gun[1] on Friday

[1] An Hour before Sunſet.

the 17th. In the Afternoon of the 16th, a Council of War was held in the General's Tent, confifting of Field Officers, (the Governor and Lieutenant Governor being prefent), to confider of a final Anfwer to be fent to the Count, when it was the unanimous Opinion of the whole Members :— That the Town fhould be defended to the laft Extremity, and that this Refolution fhould be made known to the French General.

This Day, to the inexpreffible Joy of the whole Army, the Honourable Colonel Maitland, with Part of the Troops under his Command, arrived here from Beaufort, and on Friday the 17th, fome more of them came up to Town. The Artillerymen of the Heffian Corps, Heffian Convalefcents and about 170 of the 71ft Regiment, were left with the *Vigilant*, armed Ship, three Gallies, and three Tranfports, which were obliged to remain at Dafufkee, with all the Artillery, Stores, Baggage, &c., fome of the French Frigates having got a confiderable

Way up the River. The whole of the Troops which arrived from Beaufort, amounted to about 800 Men. They were piloted up through the Marſhes, and through Daſuſkee Cut-off, where they were often up to the Middle in Mud and Water, and were brought up the River in ſmall Boats.

On the Evening of Sunday the 19th, two French Frigates appeared in Sight of the Town below Salter's Iſland. Juſt before Dark, two Rebel Gallies came farther up, and exchanged a good many Shot with the *Savannah*, *Venus* Tranſport, and the *Comet* and *Thunderer* Gallies.

The French were buſily employed in bringing Cannon, &c., from Bewlie till the 23d, when in the Night they broke Ground.

Next Morning about 90 of the Light Infantry under Major Graham, were ſent out to endeavour to bring the French out of their Lines, thereby to form ſome Judgment of their Numbers, and bring them

open to the Fire of our Cannon. The
Scheme fucceeded. Major Graham was
followed by a heavy Column of the French,
who were expofed to the Fire of the Cannon, which galled them feverely: Their
Lofs by good Authority, 14 Officers, and
145 Privates killed and wounded: Our
Lofs, 1 Subaltern and 3 Privates killed, and
15 wounded. In the Evening there was a
good deal of Firing betwixt the Enemy's
Gallies and ours.

In the Morning of Saturday the 25th,
there was a fmart Cannonade for a fhort
Time from a French Battery of one 18 and
one 6 Pounder; a Heffian was killed in his
Tent by an 18 lb. Shot. Several Balls went
through Houfes in Town, but no Perfon
was hurt. The Rebel Gallies in the Evening began again to fire at ours, which was
returned, and likewife a good many Shot
were fired at them from the Battery at the
Truftee's Gardens, where Capt. John Mills
commanded. Betwixt eight and nine at
Night, one of the Enemy's Gallies, which

came up as far as the *Roſe* Man-of-war, (ſunk on the Garden Bank), was ſoon obliged by the Fire from this Battery to be towed off to her former Station below Flyming's Iſland.

From the 24th the French were extending their Lines and Works, and bringing Cannon, Mortars, &c., from Bewlie, Thunderbolt, and Caſton's Bluff.

On Tueſday the 28th, a French armed Ship of 28 Guns, called the *Treuite*, anchored in the Back River, nearly oppoſite the Town.

Saturday Oct. 2d, about Noon, the above Ship, and the two Rebel Gallies began a heavy Fire upon the Town and Camp, which continued about an Hour, but did no Damage. During the Afternoon they fired a good deal more, as before.

On Sunday the 3d, at twelve at Night, the French opened a Bomb Battery of nine Mortars, and threw Shells into the Town and Camp all Night, one of which killed Enſign Pollard of the ſecond Battallion of Gen. De Lancey's Brigade, in a House on the Bay.

On the Morning of Monday the 4th, juſt as our Morning Gun was fired, the Enemy opened two Batteries, on which they had mounted 37 Pieces of Cannon, 18, 12, and 6 Pounders, from which they began a moſt furious Cannonade upon the Town, at the ſame Time not relaxing in their Bombardment. A young Woman, Daughter of Mrs. Thompſon, on the Bay, was killed by one of the Shot, but no Perſon was hurt in Camp. During this Cannonade and Bombardment, the Ship in the Back River, and the Rebel Gallies alſo fired many Shot into the Town. The Fire from our Batteries was alſo very hot, and many Shells from ſeven ſmall Cohorns were thrown into the French Works. This Day the Governor and Lieutenant Governor[1] moved to the Camp, having pitched a Tent next to Colonel Maitland's, on the right of the Line.

[1] Governor Sir James Wright ; Lieutenant Governor John Graham.

Tuefday, the 5th, at feven in the Morning, there was again a Cannonade and Bombardment from the Enemy. A Mulatto Man and three Negroes were killed in the Lieutenant Governor's Cellar. In the Evening the Houfe of the Late Mrs. Lloyd, near the Church, was burnt by a Shell, and feven Negroes loft their Lives in it. Whilft the Houfe was on Fire, one of the hotteft Cannonadings they had yet made was kept up to prevent People from extinguifhing the Flames. In the Night, another Shell fell through Mr. Laurie's Houfe in Broughton Street, which killed two Women and two Children who were under it. The Bombardment and Cannonade continued all Night.

Wednefday, the 6th, there was another Cannonade and Bombardment as before, which fhattered the Houfes in Town confiderably. The French opened another Battery of two fmall Guns near their Bomb Battery.

Thurfday, the 7th, the fame as the preceding Day ; feveral Carcafes were thrown during the Night, one of which burnt an old Houfe on Broughton Street.

Capt. John Simpfon, of the Georgia Loyalifts, was killed on the Morning of Friday the 8th by a Grape-fhot from one of the French Batteries, whilft he was walking in Major Wright's Redoubt. Much Damage was done this Day to the Houfes by Cannon Shot. The Firing continued very hot all Night, and a great number of Shells were thrown, one of which fell into the Provoft, killed two Men on the Spot, and wounded nine others, fome of whom died fince. Another burft in the Cellar, under the Office of the Commiffioner of Claims, killed one Negro, and wounded another.

On Saturday, the 9th, about daybreak, an Attack[1] was made by the French and

---

[1] The Britifh had been notified of the Plan of this Attack by James Curry, a Clerk of Charlefton, who had been made Ser-geant-Major of the Volunteer Grenadiers of that City, and who deferted to the Enemy. They were therefore prepared to refift the real Attack, and on their Guard againft the feint Movements of the Allies.—*Stevens's Hift. of Georgia*, ii, 215.

F

Rebels upon the Redoubt to the Right of our Lines, on the Road leading to Ebenezer,[1] the Battery near the Spring, and on the Redoubt by Colonel Maitland's Tent, into which the Colonel, Governor and Lieutenant Governor repaired.

The Attack was made with great Spirit and Impetuofity by the French, fuppofed to be about 3,500, of the Flower of their Army; to which were joined about 2,500 Rebels, confifting of the Virginia and South Carolina Continentals, and South Carolina Militia. Count D'Eftaing acted as Firft, and General Lincoln as Second in Command. The Morning being very Foggy, favored them in their Affault, which continued about an hour, when they were beat back, and moft fhamefully retreated with great Precipitation. The Troops who alone defeated this formidable Force confifted of

---

[1] A German Settlement, twenty-five Miles from Savannah. A Hofpital was eftablifhed there by the Britifh in the Revolution.

28 difmounted Dragoons,	In the Redoubts on the Ebe-
28 Battalion Men of the 60th Re-	nezer Road, where Cap-
giment,	tain Tawfe commanded,
54 South Carolina Loyalifts,	and who fell in bravely
	defending it.

90 of Col. Hamilton's North Car-	
olina Loyalifts,	In the Redoubt in which Co-
75 Militia, under Capt's Wallace,	lonel Maitland was.
Tallemach, and Polhill,	

74 Grenadiers, of the 60th Regi-	Who were ordered to fup-
ment,	port the Redoubt, and
37 Marines,	bravely charged the Ene-
	my with their Bayonets.

Befides the above, the Spring Battery of 6 Guns, manned by 31 Sailors, under the Command of Captains Manley and Stiel, did very great Execution, which contributed much to the glorious Succefs of the Day.

On the Left, the Rebels made two Feints; one on Major Wright's Redoubt by General Williamfon,[1] with 500 Men, the other on Colonel Cruger's, by General Huger,[2] with

[1] General Andrew Williamfon, whofe fubfequent Defection gave him the Title of the " Southern Arnold."

[2] General Ifaac Huger, of South Carolina.

700 men; but both Parties foon returned, having about 500 Men killed and wounded.

After the Retreat of the Enemy from our Right, 270 Men, chiefly French, were found Dead; upwards of 80 of whom lay in the Ditch and on the Parapet of the Redoubt, firft attacked, and 93 were within our Abattis. Two Rebel Standards were once fixed on the Redoubt on the Ebenezer Road; one of them was carried off again, and the other, which belonged to the Second Carolina Regiment, was taken.[1]

[1] Colonel Laurens, at the Head of the Light Infantry, the Second South Carolina Regiment, and the Firft Battalion of Charlefton Militia, alfo attacked the Redoubt; and the Colors of the Second South Carolina Regiment, which had been prefented to it by Mrs. Elliott, of Charlefton, were for a Moment planted on the Berm by Lieutenants Hume and Bufh, who being killed, Lieutenant Grey advanced to their Support; but he being mortally wounded, Sergeant Jafper rufhed forward, and, though mortally wounded, brought off his Colors at the Expenfe of his Life.—*Stevens's Hift. of Georgia*, ii, 217. The daring and fuccefsful Enterprifes of Sergeant William Jafper form fome of the moft ftriking Paffages in the Hiftory of the Southern Campaigns of the Revolution.—*Bowen's Lincoln*, p. 315; *Garden's Anecdotes*, i, 6, 77, &c. Jafper County in Georgia has fince been named in honor of this brave Sergeant.

Since the Attack, we have learnt from French Officers, Deserters and other, that they loft in killed and wounded 700 Men, fome fay 1,000, and others 1,800, reckoning 63 Officers, in the Lift of Slain. Amongft the Wounded were Count d'Eftaing and the famous Polifh Count Pulafki. The former received a Mufket-fhot in his Arm, and another in his Thigh; the latter, a Grape-fhot in his Groin, and is fince dead.[1]

---

[1] Count Pulafki, with his Cavalry, followed the attacking Columns with the View of charging in the Rear of the Redoubts at the firft vulnerable Point ; but, finding the Front of d'Eftaing's Troops thrown into Confufion by the deadly Fire of the Britifh, he left his Command to the Care of Colonel Horry, and with Captain Bentalou haftened on his black Charger to animate, by his Prefence, the wavering Spirits of the Soldiers, and carry out the Plans of d'Eftaing, now twice wounded, and borne from the Field. He dafhed on heedlefs of Danger, and anxious only to retrieve the Difcomfiture into which the head Columns had been thrown. He penetrated to the Spring Hill Redoubt — the Scene of the greateft Carnage, and, endeavoring to rally the difordered Troops, was ftruck by a Grape-fhot from the laft Gun of the Baftion. He reeled upon his Horfe which, unguided, plunged madly forward until his noble Rider fell into the Arms of his Comrades, and was borne by them back from the murderous Conflict.

But nothing human could ftand before the terrible Cannonade

Our Lofs on this ever memorable Occafion was only Capt. Tawfe, and 15 Privates

from the Enemy's Lines. Troops the braveſt, Soldiers the moſt
diſciplined, Hearts the ſtouteſt, quailed before the Angel of
Death, as he ſeemed to ſpread out his Wings upon that Blood-
covered Plain. When the ſecond American Column, under
McIntoſh, reached the Spring Hill Redoubt, the Scene of Confufion was dreadful. They marched up over Ground ſtrewn with
the Dead and Dying; and ſeldom has the Sun of a warm October Morning looked down upon a Scene ſo mournful and appaling.
The Smoke of the Muſkets and Cannon hung broodingly over
the Place, gathering denſeneſs and darkneſs from every Diſcharge;
and the Roar of Artillery, the Rattling of ſmall Arms, the calling
Bugle, the ſounded Retreat, the ſtirring Drum, and the Cries of
the Wounded blended ſtartlingly together.

Colonel Huger, marching through the low Rice Grounds,
reached his appointed Poſt, and was received with Muſic and
a briſk Diſcharge, which killed twenty-eight of his Men, and
compelled him to retreat. Only the Column of McIntoſh was
now freſh and ready for Action. But the Fate of the Day was
decided; the French and Americans had been slain and wounded
by hundreds, and their Bodies lined the Redoubts and Ditches.
They had left their Camp in anticipation of deciſive Victory,
Blood-bought and Toil-earned, indeed, but yet Victory; and
expected to Plant the Standards of the Army over the proſtrate
Enſigns of England; but the betrayal of their Plans of Attack,
and the loſing of their Way, with the conſequent Detention till
Daylight revealed their Poſition to the Enemy, changed the For-
tunes of the Day, and, though bold, valiant, and perſevering,
they were repulſed and ſlaughtered. For one Hour, they had
ſtood gallant and undaunted before the murderous Cannonade,

killed, and 35 wounded; amongft them, Lieut. Smollett Campbell of the Light Dragoons, and Lieut. James Wallace of the firft Company of Militia.[1]

Our whole Force—Regulars, Militia, Volunteers and Sailors—on Duty did not exceed 2,350 Men.

A Flag was foon fent in by the Enemy, defiring a Truce for the Burial of their Dead, and receiving the Wounded, which was agreed to till three o'clock in the Afternoon, and then prolonged till dark. During the Night there was a flight Cannonading on both Sides, and many Deferters came in.

Sunday, 10th, feveral Flags paffed, and Truces were agreed to for the above Purpofes. Some Deferters came in during the Night.

which ftruck down Rank after Rank, and fent Difmay, by its fweeping Fury, into every Column until, finding further Attempt but ufelefs Sacrifice of Life, a Retreat was ordered, and the Remains of that gallant Army were drawn off the Field.—*Stevens's Hift. of Georgia,* ii, 217.

[1] See official Report of Cafualties in the Appendix.

Monday, 11th, Deferters continued coming in, who informed that the French were fending off their Sick and Wounded, and heavy Cannon, on board their Ships; and that the Panic-ftruck Rebel Militia were running off in great numbers.

On Tuefday, the 12th, at day-light the French fired only three Shot from fmall Pieces of Cannon.

Wednefday, 13th, the Enemy, early in the Morning, fired one Shot from a Field-piece, in return for feveral from our Batteries. This Forenoon the *Truite* moved out of the Back River, and came to anchor at Five-Fathom-Hole, the Wind being unfavourable for her getting down the River. In the Night a few Shot from our Batteries produced fome from the French.

On the Night of Thurfday, the 14th, our firing was anfwered by the Enemy. Deferters ftill came in. Two more Rebel Gallies joined the others at Five-Fathom-Hole.

Friday, the 15th, we were informed that

all the Carolina Militia were gone off. This Day a Ship came up and joined the Enemy's Fleet. Deferters continued to come in. Much Firing from our Batteries in the Night, anfwered by three or four Guns from the French.

Saturday, the 16th, in the Afternoon there was a great deal of fkirmifhing on Mr. Gillivray's Plantation, betwixt fome Negroes and a Party of Rebels, and the latter were feveral Times driven from the Buildings on the Plantation into the Woods. Want of Ammunition, however, obliged the Blacks to retreat in the Evening, with the Lofs of one killed, and three or four wounded. The Enemy's Lofs is not known. There was very little firing this Night from the French, who had fent off all their Cannon except two.

Sunday, the 17th, we were informed that the French Mulatto and Black Brigade had marched to Col. Mulryne's[1] to embark. The Enemy fired a few Shot in the Night.

[1] John Mullryne.

G

Monday, the 18th, our firing this Night was not anfwered by the Enemy.

On Tuefday, the 19th, we received Advice that the French had taken Poft two Miles from Town, at the Crofs-roads, lead-ing to Brewton's,[1] with a Swamp on their Right and Left, and that the Rebels were croffing the River with all Expedition at the Two Sifters, and the Rev. Mr. Zubly's Ferry.[2] The French Batteries were this Day deftroyed by Parties fent out for that Purpofe.

Wednefday, 20th, the Militia were dif-charged; the Light Dragoons fcoured the Country, and brought in fome Prifoners. All the French embarked at Cafton's Bluff in 100 Boats, in which they proceeded to Tybee, and went on board their Ships.

From the 21ft to the 30th the Wind,

[1] Brewton's Hill was a Bluff, thirty Feet high, diftant by Road three or four Miles from the Town. A narrow Caufeway, a third of a Mile long, occurred on this Road.

[2] Rev. John J. Zubly, D.D., was at an early Period enlifted in the Continental Caufe, and was a Delegate in Congrefs; but he fubfequently gave his adherence to the Crown.

hanging to the Eaftward, prevented the Enemy's Shipping that had come up the River from getting down. Cartels during the Time were coming up with Prifoners.

The 31ft the French and Rebel Veffels got down to Cockfpur.[1]

And on Tuefday, the 2d of November, the whole of the Enemy's Shipping that were at Tybee failed over the Bar, and left our Port open.[2]

---

[1] Fort Pulafki was fubfequently erected by the United States Government on Cockfpur's Ifland, fourteen Miles below Savannah. It was begun in 1831.

[2] Profeffor Stevens, in reviewing the Events of this Siege, makes the following Remarks:

"Looking back upon the Siege of Savannah, and taking in all its Operations at one Survey, we are aftonifhed at the Number of Errors which feemed to mark the Conteft. The firft great Error was in the French Fleet paffing by Beaufort, without capturing Colonel Maitland and his eight Hundred Men. The overwhelming Force of the French could eafily have effected this, but the Charlefton Pilots refufed to take the Ships over Port Royal Bar. Had this Regiment been captured, the Fate of the City would have been reverfed. The fecond Error was in the hafty Summons of the City to furrender to the Arms of the King of France before d'Eftaing had been joined by Lincoln. The joint Summons of thefe Generals, backed by the Prefence of their joint Armies, would have produced a different Anfwer

It is not known which way the Count d'Eftaing has fteered his Courfe. It was

from the Englifh Commander. The third great Error — the fatal Error — was in the French General granting a Truce of twenty-four Hours. That Truce faved the City. It was highly impolitic, when a fudden Impreffion was defired; but it was almoft culpable, when the American General was not prefent, but was hourly expected, to concede fuch a Priviledge without his approval. D'Eftaing was too much flufhed with the Victories of Grenada and St. Vincents to be cautious. Lincoln had been too long fchooled in Difafters not to be wary and vigilant.

"The Englifh Officers themfelves acknowledged that had the combined Armies marched to Savannah at their firft Junction, they could eafily have taken it; fo poorly defenfible was it at the Beginning of the Siege. The Ignorance of their Guides, and the Betrayal of their Plan of Attack, completed the Series of Misfortunes which refulted in their Overthrow.

"The Seafon of the Year, both for Land and Sea Operations, was the moft improper which could have been chofen. Who, that is at all acquainted with our Coaft, does not know its peculiar Expofure to the equinoctial Gales of September? And who, that knows our Climate, is not aware of the almoft certain Sicknefs which, during our Fall Months, attacks the Stranger, particularly at that Period, when camping near Swamps and Ditches? The confequence was, that the French Officers and Troops, both at Sea and on Land, were continually anxious, reftive, longing to depart; fearing the Miafma on Shore and the Hurricane on the Ocean. Both came to them too foon; but the Deftruction of neither equalled the Carnage of the Battle. There was a vauntingnefs at times in the Language of d'Eftaing, faid 11 of his Line-of-battle Ships were to go with him to France, and the remainder to Chefapeak to refit and take in Provifions. Wherever they may have gone, it is to be hoped, when he is fent by the King, his Mafter, on another Expedition, fhould he have Occafion to fummon a Garrifon to furrender, and find it neceffary to vaunt of

which rendered it too haughty to be brave. His Words at his Summons — 'I have not been able to refufe the Army of the United States uniting itfelf with the King,' is a ftrange Piece of Diplomacy; for it implies that he had endeavored to prevent it, when his very Purpofe in coming to Georgia was to effect it. The Conduct of the French Troops during the Siege was exemplary and praifeworthy. A generous Emulation, and nothing more, pervaded both Armies; and the Bravery of the Allies needs no greater Comment than the Number of Dead and Wounded they left upon the Field of Battle. Wafhington, writing to General Lincoln two Months after this Attack, concerning its Failure, thus alludes to the Army : 'While I regret the Misfortune, I feel a very fenfible Pleafure in contemplating the gallant Behaviour of the Officers and Men of the French and American Army; and it adds not a little to my Confolation to learn that, inftead of mutual Reproaches, which too often follow the Failure of Enterprifes depending upon the Coöperation of Troops of different Nations, their Confidence in and Efteem for each other are increafed.' "—*Hiftory of Georgia*, ii, 223.

the valorous Deeds he performed at Grenada, where, with an Army of 4,000 Men,
he took a Fort by Storm, garrifoned with
about 80 Regulars and fome Militia, he
will keep in remembrance the Names of
General MEADOWS, and PREVOST. This
will fufficiently ferve to humble his haughty
Spirit, and convince him that he is not altogether invincible.

It is imagined the French, in this late
Bombardment, did not throw lefs than
1,000 Shells into the Town and Camp.
The Carcafes thrown were in Number
about twenty.

Laft Sunday Morning, the Brig *Three
Friends* failed for London, in which went
Paffengers Capt. Shaw, of the 60th Regiment, Aid-de-camp to his Excellency, Gen.
Prevoft, and Capt. Chriftian, Commander
of His Majefty's armed Ship *Vigilant;* alfo
failed for New York the Sloop *Crawford,*
in which Capt. Patrick Campbell, of the
71ft Regiment, went Paffenger.

We are told that one of the French flat-bottomed Boats, full of Soldiers and Sailors, when they began to land their Troops off Offabaw, in a Swell of the Sea, filled with Water, by which means fhe funk, and all on board perifhed.[1]

In confequence of a Proclamation, iffued by His Excellency the Governor, laft Friday[2] was obferved here as a Day of public Thankfgiving to Almighty God, for his very fignal Mercies vouchfafed us during the Siege of this Town, by the united Forces of the French and Rebels.

All the French and Rebel Veffels have left this River.

November 25. A Veffel arrived at St. Auguftine from Antigua, brings an Account of eleven ftore Ships, under Convoy of a 40 and a 32-Gun Ship from France, bound to Martinico, being taken by fome of our Fleet in the Weft Indies.

---

[1] Captain Henry, of the Ship *Fowey*, ftates, in a Letter publifhed in the Appendix, that the French loft one Hundred Men by this Accident.

[2] October 29, 1779.

Tuefday laft, arrived here His Majefty's Ship *Blonde*, ANDREW BARCLAY, *Efqr.*, Commander, from New York, but laft from St. Auguftine, in which came Paffenger Major Gen. LESLIE; Major Sheriff alfo came in the above Veffel from Eaft Florida.

Additions to the Journal of the Proceedings of the Victorious Army at Savannah in Georgia.

On the 23d, fome Officers' Wives were fent on Shore; they were taken on the Paffage from New York at the fame Time with the *Experiment*, Man-of-war.

On the 24th, the Comte Noailles, Nephew to the laft Ambaffador from France to our Court, with the Commander of the *Truette* Frigate, came to Savannah with the Seamen and Marines taken in the *Experiment* and *Ariel;* Sir James Wallace,[1] and Capt. Mc-

---

[1] The Journal of the *Experiment*, with an Account of her Capture, are given on a fubfequent Page of this Volume.

Kinzie being faid already to have embarked for Old France, in order to their being exchanged — there not being Officers of equal Rank to them here. The Comte declared the Panic of the Troops laft embarked was fuch, that they would have laid down their Arms had we detached 500 of our Troops to purfue them; that 63 of their Officers were killed, and 20 wounded, and 1,000 of the beft Soldiers of France, befides great Numbers by Sicknefs at their Landing; that their Effectives confifted of

Number of Effectives, - - -	3,000
Marines from their Ships, - -	1,500
Mulattoes, - - - - -	500
	5,000
The Rebels confifted of, - - -	2,500
	7,500

On the Day of the Attack, that the Returns of the Lofs of Seamen and Marines in the Engagement with Admiral Byron, off Grenada, was upwards of 700 Men;

H

that the Death of Comte Brown was
greatly lamented. Noailles added, that he
was one of the beft Officers the French
King had in his Service; that their whole
Fleet (which, on their firft Arrival, confifted of 25 Ships of the Line, 13 Frigates,
and 3 fmall-armed Veffels), are very thinly
Manned, having loft many Seamen and
Marines by Sicknefs fince the Battle with
Admiral Byron; and off Georgia, owing to
bad Provifions and bad Weather, that the
Magnifique, of 74 Guns, is fo very leaky,
that they were forced to take out her Guns,
and that fhe and the *Valiant*, of 64, have
not more than 140 Hands on board. In
fhort, the Comte de Noailles fays, that if
ten Ships of the Line were to engage them
in their prefent Condition, they would be
able to take their whole Fleet; that in
our Sortie on the 24th, the French had 17
Officers killed and wounded, and upwards
of 150 Men; that Mons. Bougainville, and
all the French Land and Sea Officers greatly
exclaimed againft Comte d'Eftaing, and alfo

at the rafcally behaviour of the Rebels on the Day of Battle.[1]

Great Honor is due to General Prevoft for his fteady, cool, and moderate Manner, in which he gave his Orders during the Siege, particularly on the Day of Attack. Our Chief Engineer, Capt. Moncrieffe, has immortalized himfelf by his indefatiguable Perfeverance in erecting and ftrengthening the Batteries, Redoubts, &c. * * * It is faid General Prevoft has made a Difpofition for the Recovery of the Poft at Beaufort, of which we doubt not the Honourable General Leflie will foon take Poffeffion.

It is with much Regret we announce the Death of Captain Eneas McIntofh,[2] Cap-

---

[1] The extreme Improbability that an Officer in the French Service fhould have willingly made fuch Difclofures of Loffes to an Enemy, leads us to regard the Statements as altogether a Fiction, and invented by the Englifh Writer of the above Article.

[2] Corrected in a fubfequent Paper to *Angus* McIntofh. There was another Officer named Eneas McIntofh ftill at Savannah. The Eftate of the Deceafed was fettled by Lachlan McIntofh, Commiffary, No. 1,078, Water Street, N. Y.

tain and Paymafter of the 71ft Regiment in Georgia.

The following is fuppofed, upon good Authority, to be the Difpofition of the Comte d'Eftaing's Fleet.

Twelve departed for Europe; five, under Mons. De Graffe, for the Weft Indies. The Remainder, four of which have loft their Rudders, are lame Ducks, and fcattered in different Parts of the Continent.

ANOTHER JOURNAL

OF THE

SIEGE OF SAVANNAH.

[From Rivington's Royal Gazette, No. 335, Dec. 15, 1779.]

SEPTEMBER 3, 1779. Saw from Tybee Light-houfe four large Ships in the Offing; fent Lieut. Lock in the Pilot Boat to reconnoitre them.

4th. The Lieutenant returned, and reported the ftrange Ships in the Offing to be two French Ships of the Line, two Frigates and a Sloop.

5th. They ftood off this Day and appeared again.

6th. Lieut. Whitworth was difpatched with Advice to New York of the Enemy being on the Coaft, but was chafed in° by the French.

7th. Lieut. Whitworth failed again, and we hope efcaped the Enemy, employed in founding the North Channel, and bringing

the *Rofe*, *Keppel* and *Germain* Men-of-war
into it, and mooring them.

8th. The Signal was made from the
Light-houfe, of feeing 18 Sail; at Sunfet
counted 41 Sail, 32 of which appeared
large Ships; an Officer and Reinforcement
came to Tybee Fort, which had only one
24-pounder, and one 8½-inch Howitzer.
Came down from Cockfpur, and anchored
in the North Channel.   His Majefty's Ship
Fowey, the *Savannah* armed Ship, Tranfports and Prifon Ships, ready to go up to
Savannah River.   Started all the Water
except the Ground Tier.

9th. At Daylight, faw the French Fleet,
fome of them in Chafe of a Schooner with
Englifh Colours, which they took.

10th. Four of the Enemy's Ships got
under Way at high Water, and ftood for
Tybee; the *Fowey* made the Signal to
weigh; weighed with the *Fowey*, *Keppel*
and *Comet* Galley, and run up Savannah
River as far as Long Beach.   The *Fowey*
got aground on White Vefter Bank.   Or-

dered the *Keppel* and *Comet* to her Affiftance, with Boats, Anchors, &c. The Fort
was abandoned and burnt. The French
Ships anchored off Tybee. The *Fowey* got
off at high Water.[1]

[1] The following Orders were iffued September 9th:

"The Regiment of Wiffenbach to take their Ground of Encampment; likewife the 2d Battalion of General Delancey's.
In Cafe of an Alarm, which will be known by the beating to
Arms, both at the Barracks and main Guard, the Troops are to
repair to their feveral Pofts without Confufion or Tumult.

"Captain Stuart, of the Britifh Legion, will take Poft with
his Men on the Right, near the River.

"The Main Guard to be relieved by Convalefcents from the
Heffians.

"Major Wright's Corps to fend their Convalefcents in the
old Fort. Twenty-four Men in the fmall Redoubt, and feventy
Men in the Left Flank Redoubt, upon the Road to Tatnall's.

"The Militia to affemble in Rear of the Barracks.

"The Light Infantry, the Dragoons, and Carolina Light-
horfe, as a Referve, two hundred Yards within the Barracks.

"The King's Rangers, commanded by Lieutenant Colonel
Brown, in the fmall Redoubt on the Right, with fifty Men; the
Remainder extending towards the larger Redoubt on the Right.

"The Carolinians, divided equally in the two large Redoubts.

"The Battalion Men of the 60th Regiment in the right Redoubt, the Grenadiers on the Left, extending along the Abatis

11th. Employed founding and laying off the Channel leading to Savannah. The *Fowey*, *Keppel*, and *Comet* Galley anchored there.

12th. At Sunfet a French Ship anchored off Tybee ; two more anchored in the South Channel, and one in the North. Perceived fhe was aground.

13th. At 2 P. M. a Sloop, the *Crawford*,

towards the Barracks; the Heffians on their Left, fo as to fill up the Space to the Barracks.

"On the Left of the Barracks, the 3d Battalion of Skinner's, General Delancey's, and the New York Volunteers; and on their Left the 71ft Regiment, lining the Abatis to the left Flank Redoubt, on the Road to Tatnall's.

"If all the Orders are filently and punctually obeyed, the General makes no doubt that if the Enemy fhould attempt to make an Attack but that they will be repulfed, and the Troops maintain their former well acquired Reputation. Nor will it be the firft Time that Britifh and Heffian Troops have beat a greater Superiority, both French and Americans, than it is probable they will have to encounter on this Occafion. The General repeats his firm Reliance on the Spirit and fteady Coolnefs of the Troops he has the Honour to Command."—*Stevens's Hift. of Georgia*, ii, 203.

The original Order Book of General Prevoft was in Poffeffion of J. K. Tefft, Efq., of Savannah, when quoted by Mr. Stevens.

came along-fide. Sent eight 9-Pounders, 400 Shot, and eight Barrels of Powder, &c., to the Army. The *Comet* Galley moved to Cockfpur and exchanged fome Shot with the French Ships aground—the French Fleet at anchor without the Bar. At 7 A. M., weighed, as did the *Fowey, Keppel,* and *Comet* Galley. At half paft, the Ship took the Ground, but foon floated. Anchored with the fmall Bower. At 8 weighed, and came up the River. At 11 anchored at Five-Fathom-Hole.

14th. Sent Lieut. Lock 26 Seamen, Capt. Rankin, and all the Marines to reinforce the Army, per Order from Commodore Henry.

15th. At 2 the *Keppel* and *Comet* went down the Harbour to cover and protect the Troops expected from Beaufort. This Day I joined the Army with the remaining Part of the Officers and Ship's Company, leaving only enough to keep the Ship free. Pofted the Officers and Seamen to the different

I

Batteries in the Line. The General received a Summons from Count d'Eſtaing[1] to ſurrender, &c., &c., TO THE ARMS OF THE FRENCH KING. A Council of War was

[1] Charles Hector Comte d'Eſtaing was born in Auvergne in 1729; began his military Career as a Colonel of Infantry, and ſoon after, being advanced to the Rank of Brigadier, was ſent, under Count de Lally, to ſerve in the Eaſt Indies. He was taken Priſoner at Madras in 1759, and paroled, but had the Indiſcretion to violate his Pledge; and, upon again falling into the Hands of the Engliſh, was treated with great Severity. He lay in cloſe Confinement a long Time in the Hulks at Portſmouth, but was finally releaſed. At the Peace of 1763 he was made Lieutenant-General of the naval Forces; but his Appointment occaſioned Jealouſies in the Navy which he never overcame.

In 1778 he was ſent as Vice-Admiral to America with twelve Ships; but adverſe Winds detained him till Lord Howe, with a much ſmaller Squadron in the Delaware, had reëmbarked, and landed his Troops in New York. When before Rhode Iſland, and about to attack the Britiſh, a Storm ſcattered and diſabled his Fleet. His ſubſequent Succeſs in the Weſt Indies, and Failure before Savannah are noticed in theſe Pages. After this Repulſe, he returned to France. In 1783, he commanded a French and Spaniſh Fleet at Cadiz, but the Peace put an End to this Expedition.

Entering with Spirit into the French Revolution, he became, in 1789, Commandant of the National Guard at Verſailles; but his Career was not without grievous Stains upon his Name, and he periſhed under the Guillotine in April, 1794, under the Charge of being a counter Revolutioniſt.

called on the Occafion, and an Anfwer was
fent. A Trooper of Pulafki's was brought
in this Morning.

16th. The Remainder of the *Rofe* and
Fowey's Guns were landed. The Guns were
immediately mounted on the different Batteries. Colonel Maitland, and the Troops
from Beaufort arrived — 71ft and New
York Volunteers; brave Fellows. Savannah in the higheft Spirits.[1]

[1] The Refult of the impending Attack was doubtlefs decided
by this Arrival.

"Every Avenue by which the Approach of Col. Maitland
and his Highlanders could be looked for was clofed; yet by un-
conquerable Induftry, he difcovered an obfcure Creek, but little
navigated; and, by dint of perfevering Exertion, dragging his
Boats through it, reached the Garrifon before the Time allowed
for Deliberation had expired. Entering the Council Chamber
where Difcuffions were carrying on, he is faid to have approached
with hurried Step the Table, and, ftriking the Hilt of his Clay-
more againft it, to have exclaimed, 'the Man who utters a Sylla-
ble recommending Surrender, makes me his decided Enemy; it
is neceffary that either *he* or *I* fhould fall.' So refolute a Speech,
at a Moment fo critical, produced the happieft Effect on the
Minds of all. Hope and Courage regained their Influence in every
Mind; each Individual repaired to his Poft with Alacrity and
Confidence; the Terms offered by the Befiegers were rejected,

17th. A Truce agreed on for 24 Hours, viz., till Gun-fire, P. M.[1]

18th. Continued Truce.

19th. Hands fent down to bring the Ships up nearer the Town. All the Ships

and the Town was faved."—*Garden's Anecdotes of the American Revolution*, Brooklyn Ed. 1865, iii, 101.

[1] The following Orders of the Day, for the 17th of September, indicate the Spirit with which the Englifh Commander engaged in the impending Conteft:

"GENERAL ORDERS.

"Camp before Savannah,—17th September, 1779.

"Parole — *Maitland*.   Counterfign — *St. George*.

"Field Officers for To-morrow — Lieutenant Colonel Cruger and Major Graham.

"The Troops to be under Arms this Afternoon at four o'clock; as the Enemy is now very near, an Attack may be hourly expected; the General therefore defires that the whole may be in inftant readinefs. By the known Steadinefs and Spirit of the Troops, he has the moft unlimited Dependance, doubting nothing of a glorious Victory, fhould the Enemy try their Strength. What is it that may not, by the Bleffing of God, be expected from the united Efforts of Britifh Sailors and Soldiers, and valliant Heffians, againft an Enemy that they have often beat before? In Cafe of a Night Attack, the General earneftly requefts the utmoft Silence to be obferved, and Attention to the Officers, who will be careful that the Men do not throw away their Fire at random, and warn them earneftly not to fire until ordered."—*Stevens's Hift. of Georgia*, ii, 311.

moved; the Pickets firing moſt Part of the Night.

20th. New Works thrown up, the French Ship Rebel Galleys moving up the River. Orders from Capt. Henry to ſcuttle and ſink the *Roſe* Man-of-War in the Channel, which was immediately done, after getting out as many of her Stores, &c., as the Time would admit. The *Savannah* arm'd Ship, and *Venus*, Tranſport, were burnt, with their Guns and Proviſions, Ammunition, &c. Two or three Tranſports ſunk at Five-Fathom-Hole, or thereabouts, with all their Sails burnt, &c., &c.

21ſt. Two Negros, deſerted from the Enemy, report them Strong; Gen. Lin-coln with the Rebel Army having joined the French, and that they are preparing to attack; ſtrengthening our Works; firing occaſionally on the Enemy to diſturb them.

22d. The Enemy ſtill opening Works to the Left; fired on them occaſionally from the Batteries.

23d. Strengthening the Works, and throwing up Intrenchments in Front of the different Corps in that Line.

24th. At feven in the Morning, faw the Enemy very bufy intrenching themfelves to the Left of the Barracks. Three Companies of Light Infantry made a Sortie with great Spirit. The Enemy being too numerous, obliged them to retreat under the Fire of our Batteries, with the lofs of 21 killed and wounded. Lieut. McPherfon, of the 71ft, was killed. It is fuppofed the Enemy fuffered confiderably. The Enemy fired feveral Cannon in our Line from two 18-Pounders, and fome 4-Pounders. A Flag was fent to bury the Dead, on both Sides. In the Afternoon the Enemy's Gallies advanced near the Works. Our Gallies exchanged feveral Shots with them, and returned under the Sea Battery. The new Battery behind the Barracks finifhed this Day, mounted with two 18-Pounders, two 9-Pounders, and Field-Pieces. Throwing up Intrenchments in Front of the different Corps in the French Lines, about

half a Muſket Shot from our Abattis. The
Pickets exchanged Shot the greater Part of
the Night; we throwing Shells into their
Works, and firing on them from our Batteries every fifteen Minutes.

25th. The French throw up new Works
on the Left of the Barracks, in which they
mounted two 18-Pounders en barbette, but
were driven from them by our Batteries.
In the Evening the Rebel Gallies advanced
up to the *Roſe*, but were obliged to retire,
by the Fire of the *Comet* and *Thunderer*
Gallies. Continued throwing Shells, and
firing on their Works during the Night.

26th. At 11, A. M., the Enemy's Gallies
fired a few Shot at the Fort on the Left
of the Encampment, without Effect. A
French Frigate advanced to Five-Fathom-
Hole.

27th. At 3, A. M., a ſmall Fire of Muſ-
ketry from the Pickets. At 8, A. M., a Flag
from the French, with private Letters from
the Britiſh Priſoners. Deſtroyed the Barracks, and carried off the Wood, &c., leaving

the lower Part as a Breaftwork, to prevent it being fired from the Enemy. Continued throwing Shells, and cannonading the Enemy's Works during the Night.

28th. At 1 in the Morning a fmall firing between the Picquets. A Rebel taken clofe to our Abattis. About 2, another firing from our Picquets. At 9, A. M., a French Frigate moved up the Back River, and moored her Stern and Head. Everything quiet this Day. The Enemy carrying on their Works. 8, P. M., the *Thunderer* Galley moored near the French Frigate, and began to cannonade her. The Frigate did not return her Fire.

29th. At Daylight this Morning, faw a new Intrenchment on the Left, raifed during the Night by the Enemy, within half a Mufket Shot of our Lines. Employed throwing up Breaftworks to the Right and Left of the Barracks. Fired on the Enemy's Works every fifteen Minutes from the Batteries and Howitzers during the Night.

30th. At Daylight perceived the Enemy working and extending their Intrenchments. At 7, A. M., the *Thunderer* Galley advanced towards the French Frigate on the Back River, and fired at her. She did not return a Shot. The *Thunderer* returned, having broke the Platform of her Gun. At 10, A. M., a Brig came up to Five-Fathom-Hole. The Rebel Gallies on their former Station, near the Works below. The *Rofe*, a Boat with a fmall Gun, fired at the *Thunderer* without effect; a Launch and another Boat went up the Back River. A Man came in from the Enemy; gives no fatisfactory Intelligence. Some firing from the Battery on the Right, and the armed Veffels, on the Enemy at Yamacraw, as well as from the Batteries in the Front and the Left, on the French Intrenchments. This Night, an Officer of Pulafki's was wounded and brought into the Lines by the Picquets.

October 1ft. At 7, A. M., the French Frigate in the Back River fired fome Shot

K

towards the Town, and at the Negroes on Hutchinſon's Iſland. Perceived the Enemy in Front and on the Left, having in their Works Embraſures, &c. A Flag from us to the French, with Letters from the wounded Officer taken laſt Night. Still employed in ſtrengthening our Lines, particularly in Front. Sent out of the Lines two Dragoons of Pulaſki Legion by a Flag, who had been detained ſome Time here, and received an Officer of the ſame Legion with a Flag, *Mons. Bentoloſa,* who came to ſee the Officer that was wounded and brought in laſt Night. Employed in ſtrongly throwing up a new Battery on our Left, to be mounted with eight 9-Pounders, to act on the Enemy's Batteries. In hourly expectation of the Attack. This Afternoon freſh Breezes from E.N.E. and Rain. Fired during the Night from the Batteries in Front, and threw ſome Shells into the French Intrenchments.

2d. Rainy Weather; Wind E.N.E.; the Enemy ſtill working in their Intrenchments, and preparing the Batteries. At Noon the Enemy's Gallies advanced near the Sea Battery, and began to cannonade, as did the Frigate in the Back River. Several of their Shot came into the Rear of the Camp, and without doing Execution. The *Thunderer* returned a few Shot; the Sea Battery did not. A Deferter from Pulafki's Legion reports the Enemy's Batteries to be near ready. A Deferter from the French likewife with the fame Account. The Frigate in the Back River fired again in the Afternoon without effect. Threw Shells, and fired from the Batteries into the French Intrenchments, to difturb them during the Night.

3d. Rainy Weather; Wind E.N.E.; the Enemy ftill working in the Intrenchments, and compleating their Batteries; the French Frigate firing on the Rear of the Camp without effect. At 12 o'clock this Night, the Enemy opened the Bomb Batteries, and fired warmly into the Town, but none into the Field.

4th. The Enemy ſtill continue their Fire from the Bomb and other Batteries. It was returned by us.

5th. The Enemy ſtill cannonading the Camp and Town. At Night a Houſe took fire, but it went out without communicating to any other Building. The Frigate and Gallies firing as uſual. Heard a cannonade at Sea.

6th. The Enemy ſtill firing on the Works, Camp and Town. The Line turned out at Dawn, on an Alarm that the Enemy were approaching. The Cannonade and Bombardment continued all Night.

7th. Still continued Cannonading and throwing ſhells on both Sides; the Enemy throwing moſt of their Fire towards the Town, which ſuffers conſiderably. A 9-Pounder in our Battery, to the Right of the Barracks, burſt, and wounded a Seaman. Carpenter employed in repairing the Ebenezer Battery, which had been broke by the Enemy's Shells. At 7 at Night the Enemy threw feveral Carcafes into the Town, and burnt one Houfe.

8th. The Enemy fired little this Morning, but during the Night cannonaded and bombarded the Town furioufly.

9th. At Drum-beating in the Morning, the French attacked us warmly on the Right, and endeavoured to ftorm the Redoubt and Ebenezer Battery. The Grenadiers of the 60th Regiment advanced to fupport them, and, after an obftinate Refiftance by the French, they drove them back with great Slaughter. Their Lofs is reported to be 600 or 700 killed, wounded, and Prifoners; our Lofs, Captain Tawes, of the Dragoons, who died nobly fighting on the Parapet of the Redoubt; 7 of the 60th killed and wounded, and two Marines killed and four wounded. A Flag from the French, to bury their Dead, which was granted. At 8 at Night the French beat a Parley, but were refufed by us. They fired Cannon and Shells during the Night without any other Effect than deftroying the Houfes.

10. This Morning fent a Flag to bury their Dead. The Rebels fent one for the fame Purpofe. The Truce lafted from ten till four, p. m. The French fired feveral Cannon when it expired. Between 8 and 9, p. m., our Picquets fired on the Right feveral Shot. The Lines lay on their Arms all Night, and the Seamen ftood to their Cannon. No other firing from either Side during the Night.

11th. This Morning very Foggy. No Alarm from the Enemy. Our Line very alert and in high Spirits. The French and Rebels fent in Flags of Truce the greateft Part of the Day; the Enemy employed burying their Dead, carrying off their Wounded, and fearching for their Miffing. The French take off all their Cannon and Mortars during the Night, leaving only fome fmall Field-pieces to amufe us. Our whole Lines in Spirits, ready for another Attack. Several Defert-

ers, French and Rebels, came in, and all
report that the Enemy are moving, and
that their Lofs in the Attack is much more
than we imagined. The Rebels mifs 1,300;
the French Lofs uncertain, but greater than
the Rebels, as they fought like Soldiers,
and were killed and wounded; but the
Rebels' lofs is from Defertion immediately
after the Defeat.

12th. The French amufed us with four
Cannon Shot at Daybreak. More Deferters
came in; fay they are retreating. Count
d'Eftaing was at the Attack, and was dangeroufly wounded in two Places, and the
Flower of the French Army killed or
wounded; Count Pulafki mortally wounded.
The Enemy very quiet all Night. Opened
a new Battery on the Right, of three 4-
Pounders.

13th. We fired a Gun at 2 in the Morning. The French returned the Shot. The
whole Line very alert and under Arms. A
Flag out at nine, to return the wounded
French Officers and Soldiers. The Frigate

in the Back River moved down at high water. Heard feveral Guns from the Sea, which we fuppofe Signals. More Deferters come in, who reported the Enemy's Lofs to be great. The Rebel Militia are moftly gone off, and the Reft difpirited and ready to March to Charles Town. Our Batteries in Front fired on the Enemy's Works at Intervals during the Night. The Enemy returned the Fire, which feemed to come from one Gun. Nothing more material during the Night.

14th. More Deferters from the French and Rebels, who make the fame Report as the Former. At nine this Morning a Flag out, to fettle an Exchange of Prifoners. Some Information gives us Reafon to expect a vigorous Attack from the French as foon as they have got off their heavy Baggage, Cannon, Sick and Wounded. We fired at Times during the Night on the Enemy's Works. They returned two Shot only from two fmall Pieces, fuppofed to be 6-Pounders.

The Enemy very quiet this Morning. We could not hear the Rebels' Revielle. The French beat Drums, but fired no Morning Gun. A Light-fhip come to Five-Fathom-Hole, fuppofe for Water. Two Gallies joined the two former ones. More Deferters come in, and report the Enemy to be on the Retreat; that their Lofs the Morning of the Engagement was very great, particularly in their beft Officers. They are very fickly, and difcontented with the Rebels. The Regiment Darmagnac are on their March to Bewlie, with Baggage, Sick and Wounded. The Night quiet; firing occafionally from the Grand Battery on the Enemy's Intrenchments. They returned three or four Shot.

16th. The French beat the Revielle; the Rebels did not. More Deferters from the French, confirming the former Reports of their great Lofs and Retreat. We are, however, on our Guard. The Frigates in the River loofe their Top-fails as we fuppofe, to drop down and cover the Retreat

L

of the French.   An Alarm at Sunſet that
the Enemy are forming in our Front; the
Lines under Arms.   The Rebels ſet Fire
to ſome Houſes on our Right, as well as in
our Front.   Our armed Negroes ſkirmiſh-
ing with the Rebels the whole Afternoon.
We fired occaſionally during the Night on
the Enemy's Works and Camp.   They returned two Shot.

17th. The French beat the Revielle; the
Rebels did not.   Heard the Report of ſeveral Cannon.   A Manager of Sir James
Wright's, from Ogeeche, reports that the
Enemy were preparing to retreat; that they
loſt, the Day of the Attack, 1,500 Men
killed and wounded, and the Deſertion very
great.   Fire as uſual at the Enemy's Works.
They returned three Shot.

18th. The French beat the Reveille; the
Rebels did not, but they were heard working in the Woods.   The armed Negroes
brought in two Rebel Dragoons and eight
Horſes, and killed two Rebels who were
in a foraging Party.   Only one Deſerter

this Day from the French, who gives the fame Account as the former ones. Many Boats obferved paffing from the Enemy's Veffels and their Army. Nothing material during the Night. We fired as ufual on their Works, and they returned three Shot from a 6-Pounder. Our Lines very alert, and generally on their Arms, ready to receive the Enemy.

19th. The French beat the Revielle; the Rebels not, but we heard cutting in the Woods. The Ship that came to Five-Fathom-Hole moved down the River, as we fuppofed, full of Water, and the French Baggage.

20th. The French beat the Revielle; but did not fire the Morning Gun. Two Deferters that came in this Day, fay the Rebels marched off Yefterday Evening, after having fired their Camp. The Frigate fell down lower, but the wind being againft her could not go further.

Extract of a Letter from a Gentleman of the General Hospital at Savannah, to his Friend in this City, dated November 24, 1779.

"I NEVER began, my dear Tom, to write a Letter in better Humor. You have, no doubt, already heard of Count D'Estaing having landed 4,397 Troops in this Province, and demanding a Surrender of this Town and Garrison. Being denied, he besieged it by regular Approaches, with the coöperation of the Rebel Army, under Lincoln, amounting to 5,518 effective Men. On the Morning of the 4th of October, their Batteries were finished and opened with the Dawn. Their Cannon were well served, and kept a severe and constant fire till 11 o'clock, A. M. The Night preceding, they opened a Bomb Battery. I counted 187 Shells thrown into Town from it, with little Effect. This Amusement we had till the GLORIOUS Morning of the 9th of October. An Hour before Day the Attack began with a Feint on our Left, the main

Body upon the Right. They ſtormed
twice, but were repulſed with great Loſs.
Repulſed by whom? By 349 South Carolinians, and 24 diſmounted Horſemen! the
whole under the Command of the immortal
Capt. Tawes, to whoſe ſacred Memory,
while my Recollection of his unequalled
Merit lives, I'll pay an anniverſary Tribute.
The Peace of Heaven be with him.

The French loſt 67 Officers killed, and
594 Privates, killed and wounded. The
Rebels loſt 633. D'Eſtaing is wounded in
the Arm and Leg—not mortally. Pulaſki
is dead of his Wounds, and was thrown
overboard on their Paſſage to Charles
Town. We were two Days employed in
burying their Dead. The Morning of the
Attack, I had Charge of a 9-Pounder with
Capt. Brown,[1] of the *Roſe*, and believe me,
Tom, I never was happier in my Life than
upon this Occaſion."

[1] The Death of Capt. Brown is noticed in the *Royal Gazette*,
December 18, 1779.

*Letter from T. W. Moore[1] upon the Siege of
Savannah.*

[From Rivington's Royal Gazette, No. 339, Dec. 29, 1779.]

Savannah, 4th Nov., 1779.

* * "YOU will fee a full Account of what has been doing here; and as I know you wifh to hear how Matters went, I will give you a concife Account of the moft material Circumftances.

"Count d'Eftaing's Fleet appeared off the Bar the 4th of September, faid to be 46 in all—25 of them Ships of the Line; and came to anchor the 9th, and foon began to land their Men and Guns, and were bufy in bringing every Force againft us till the 16th, when they appeared within 300 Yards of our Lines—upwards of 4,000 French, and 3,000 Rebels. They fent in a Flag, and demanded the Town. General Prevoft defired twenty-four Hours to confider, in which Time we were reinforced

---

[1] One of the Aids-de-Camp of Gen. Prevoft. The Letter was addreffed to his Wife.

with 800 Men, under the Command of
Colonel Maitland, from Carolina. This
made us about 2,000 ftrong, and fo very
faucy as to refufe to let *Monfieur* and *Jona-
than* in.

"The Enemy began to encamp on the
22d to break Ground within 200 Yards of
our Centre, and we kept amufing them
with our great Guns, fo that they could
fcarce work in the Day Time. On the
24th, a Sortie of the Light Infantry, with
150 Men, was made on the French Intrenchments to make them fhew themfelves, which they did on our Lads firing
in upon them, and retreating back full
fpeed; and at that Inftant our Batteries
kept a conftant Fire on the Enemy, and
killed (from their own Account) upwards
of 90 Men. We loft but one Officer and
three Men. That fame Night, the French
and Rebels got fighting with one another
thro' Miftake, and 'tis faid upwards of 130
killed before they difcovered what they
were about. From this Time to the 2d

Day of October there was no firing from
the Enemy, but we kept conftantly amufing
them with Shot and Shell, by Day and
Night, that did great Execution.

"This Morning, the 2d of October, as
we fired our Morning Gun, they opened
one of the moft tremendous Firings I ever
heard; from 37 Pieces of Cannon — moftly
18-Pounders, and 9 Mortars, in Front, and
fixteen Pieces of Cannon from the River,
on our Left — moftly 24-Pounders. The
Town was torn to Pieces, and nothing but
Shrieks from Women and Children to be
heard. Many poor Creatures were killed
in trying to get in their Cellars, or hide
themfelves under the Bluff of Savannah
River. The Firing lafted for fome Hours,
and a Flag was fent from us to Count
d'Eftaing, to allow Time for the Women
and Children to go to an Ifland out of
Danger. 'Twas favagely refufed; and that
Night they began to fire again, and heave
Carcafes and red Shot, which fet two Houfes
on fire, and burnt them down; but fome

proper Perfons being appointed to extinguifh the Bombs, did it very effectually, and prevented any further Conflagration. From this Time till the 9th, we kept firing by way of Amufement at each other; but on that Morning, juft before Day, our Lines were attacked from Right to Left, and it was not many Minutes before we found the real Storm was to the Right, on a Redoubt called the Carolina Redoubt; and as I had the Honour of being one of General Prevoft's Aids-de-Camp during the Siege, I was ordered to hafte to a Redoubt manned by the Militia, to hearten them up. This was about 200 Yards from the Scene of Action.

"I found thefe brave Tories full of Spirit, ready to pour upon the Enemy (who were firing on them at too great a Diftance to kill) in Cafe they came within their Shot. On being convinced the Attack was not a Feint, I pufhed on and arrived juft as Victory had declared in our Favor; and fuch a Sight I never faw before. The Ditch

M

was filled with Dead, and in Front, for 50
Yards, the Field was covered with Slain.
Many hung dead and wounded on the
Abattis; and for fome hundred Yards with-
out the Lines, the Plain was ftrewed with
mangled Bodies, killed by our Grape and
Langridge.[1]

"I pofted back to my General (who is as
brave as Cæfar), and gave him the pleafing
Account. Soon after a Flag came from
d'Eftaing for Liberty to bury their Dead,
and requefted their Wounded. 'Twas
granted. Another Flag came from General
Lincoln, who commanded the Rebels, for
the fame Purpofe, which was alfo granted;
and that whole Day was taken up in this
Service. The Attack *in earneft*, or more
properly fpeaking, *the Storm*, was with
1,800 chofen Men, from every Regiment
of French and Rebels, led by d'Eftaing,
and many of the Nobility of France. General McIntofh[2] commanded the Rebel Col-

---

[1] Langrel, a kind of Chain-fhot, formed of Bolts, Nails, and
Pieces of Iron faftened together.

[2] General Lachlan McIntofh.

umn; but finding a very warm Reception, he prudently put to the Right-about, not without a great Lofs; as, from the Account of Deferters, the Rebels loft over 500. The French honeftly own they have loft in killed 800, and many wounded. D'Eftaing is wounded in two Places very badly. Pulafki was thought dangeroufly fo, now dead. Many French Officers of diftinction killed, as well as Rebels. I faw my old Friend, Charles Mott, a Major, among the Dead, but recollected no other quondam Acquaintance.

"From this Time to the 20th October, we amufed each other with Shot and Shells; and on that Morning we' found the Enemy had deferted their Lines and gone off. Much Credit is due to this little Army, and I hope they will have it. Poor Pollard, my Affiftant, was killed the 4th of October by an 18-Pounder, my fine valuable Negro Carpenter the 7th, and a beautiful Mare that coft me 20 Guineas; my Store of Wine, all broke by Shot and Shells, and my Quarters torn to Pieces; but this is Neighbor's Fate, and the whole Town is in the fame State.

"Be it remembered that not more than 150 in the Redoubt, and 60 Grenadiers of the 60th, who had mounted the Walls, defeated this combined Force of 1,800 chofen Men, who attacked the weakeft Part of our whole Lines; indeed, two Batteries, manned by the gallant Tars of old England, kept a conftant Blaze to the Right and Left on the Enemy, and greatly contributed to the Honour of the Day—the glorious 9th of October.

"As this Account is not for the Prefs, I fhall fay nothing of Individuals, more than that everybody behaved well.

"Killed and Wounded on our Side during the Siege, 163."

T. W. MOORE.

Summons of Count D'Eſtaing.

BY AUTHORITY.

THE Following is a faithful Tranſlation of the Compte d'Eſtaing's SUMMONS, ſent to Major General Prevoſt, requiring a Surrender of the Town of Savannah to the KING OF FRANCE.

"Count d'Eſtaing ſummons his Excellency General Prevoſt, to ſurrender himſelf to the Arms of his Majeſty the King of France: He admoniſhes him, that he will be perſonally anſwerable, for every Event and Misfortune attending a Defence, demonſtrated abſolutely impoſſible and uſeleſs, from the Superiority of the Force which attacks him by Land and by Sea. He alſo warns him, that he will be *nominally* and perſonally anſwerable, henceforward; for the burning previous to, or at the Hour of the Attack, of any Ships or Veſſels of War, or Merchant Ships in the Savannah River, as well as of Magazines in the Town.

"The Situation of the MORNE DE L'HOS-
PITAL, in Grenada, the Strength of the
three Redoubts, which defended it, the
Difproportion betwixt the Number of the
French Troops now before Savannah, and
the inconfiderable Detachment which took
Grenada by Affault, fhould be a Leffon for
the Future. Humanity requires that Count
d'Eftaing fhould remind you of it. After
this he can have no Reproach to make to
himfelf. Lord McCartney had the good
Fortune to efcape in Perfon, on the firft
Onfet of Troops, forcing a Town Sword
in Hand, but having fhut up his valuable
Effects in a Port deemed impregnable by
all his Officers and Engineers, it was im-
poffible for Count d'Eftaing to be happy
enough to prevent the whole being pillaged.
                "Signed   ESTAING."[1]

[1] The Continuation of this Correfpondence will be found in
the Appendix.

CORRESPONDENCE BETWEEN THE BRITISH
AND ALLIED COMMANDERS, AT SAVAN-
NAH.

[From Rivington's Royal Gazette, No. 358, March 4, 1780.]

*Copy of a Letter from Major General Prevoſt
to Count d'Eſtaing, ſome Days previous to
the Attack upon that Place, with his Anſwer thereto, and that of the Rebel General
Lincoln.*

Camp Savannah, 6th Oct., 1779.

SIR,

I AM perſuaded your Excellency will do
me the Juſtice to believe, that I conceive, in defending this Place, and the Army
committed to my Charge, I fulfil what is
due to Honor and Duty to my Prince.
Sentiments of a different Kind, occaſion
the Liberty of now addreſſing myſelf to
your Excellency; they are thoſe of Humanity. The Houſes of Savannah are occupied ſolely by Women and Children.
Several of them have applied to me, that I
might requeſt the Favour you would allow

them to embark on board a Ship or Ships, and go down the River under the Protection of yours, until the Bufinefs is decided. If this Requifition you are fo good as to grant, my Wife and Children, with a few Servants, fhall be the Firft to profit by the Indulgence.

I have the Honour to be, with proper Refpect, Sir, Your Excellency's moft obedient and humble Servant.

A. PREVOST.

His Excellency,
    Count d'Eftaing, &c., &c.

Reply to the Foregoing Letter.

Camp before Savannah, Oct. 6, 1779.

SIR,

WE are perfuaded that your Excellency knows all that your Duty prefcribes; perhaps your Zeal has already interfered with your Judgment.

The Count d'Eftaing, in his own Name, notified to you, that you would be perfon-

ally and alone refponfible for the Confe-
quences of your Obftinacy. The Time
which you informed him, in the Commencement of the Siege, would be neceffary for the Arrangement of Articles
including different, Orders of Men in your
Town, had no other Objeƈt than that of
receiving Succor. Such Conduƈt, Sir, is
fufficient to forbid every Intercourfe between us, which might occafion the leaft
Lofs of Time; befides, in the prefent Ap-
plication, latent Reafons might again exift;
there are military ones, which in frequent
Inftances have prevented the Indulgence
you requeft. It is with Regret we yield
to the Aufterity of our Funƈtions; and we
deplore the Fate of thofe Perfons who will
be Viƈtims of your Conduƈt, and the De-
lufion which appears to prevail in your
Mind.[1]

[1] This Refufal was probably occafioned by the Faƈt, that
General Prevoft had himfelf aƈtually denied a fimilar Applica-
tion, made by General McIntofh, in behalf of his Wife and
Family, and fuch other Females as might choofe to avail themfelves of his Courtefy.—Stevens's *Hift. Georgia*, ii, 214.

N

We are, with Refpect, Sir, Your Excellency's moft obedient Servants,

> B. Lincoln,
> D'Estaing.

His Excellency,
  Major General Prevoft.

Lift of French Forces at Savannah.

THE following is handed about as a Lift of the French Force employed againft this Province on their late Expedition:

Ships.			Guns.	Ships.			Guns.
Languedoc,	-	-	90	Hector,	-	-	74
Tonant,	-	-	80	Marfellois,	-	-	74
Robufte,	-	-	74	Vaillant,	-	-	64
Cæfar,	-	-	74	Sphinx, -	-	-	64
Annibal,	-	-	74	Recole,	-	-	64
Fendant,	-	-	74	Fantafque,	-	-	64
Dauphin Royal,		-	74	Reflechi,	-	-	64
Zele, -	-	-	74	Provence,	-	-	64
Magnifique,	-	-	74	Artefien,	-	-	64
Vengeur,	-	-	74	Sagitaire,	-	-	50
Guerrier,	-	-	74	Fier, -	-	-	50
Triumph, -		-	74	Fortune,	-	-	36

Ships.			Guns.	Ships.			Guns.
Amazon,	-	-	39	Truite,	-	-	26
Iphygenie,	-	- 36		Lively, -	-	-	20
Blance,	-	- , 32		Ceres,	-	-	18
Boudeufe,	-	- 32		Fleur de la Mere,	-	16
Chimere,	-	-	26	Alert,	-	-	12
Ellis,	-	-	- 26	Barrington,	-	-	8

With feveral unarmed Sloops and Schooners
for debarking Troops.

Land Forces.

600 of the Regiment of Anhalt.

600 of the Regiment of Auxerrois.

500 of the Regiment of Dillon.

1,000 of the Regiment of the Cape.

700 Martinico Volunteers.

1,000 of the Cape Regiment of Color.

1,000 of the Corps of Marines.

400 Volunteers.

Total, 5,800

BURLESQUE LETTER, ATTRIBUTED TO A FRENCH OFFICER.

[From Rivington's Royal Gazette, No. 343, Jan. 12, 1780.]

THE following was Yefterday brought to Town by a Gentleman from Rhode Ifland. The Original was found on board the Sloop from Georgia, which went into that Harbour after the Britifh had left it:

Extract of a Letter from a French Officer off Tybee Ifland, to his Friend in Charles Town, dated October 21, 1779.

"The Count d'Eftaing is the Wonder of the Age. Cæfar and Alexander were nothing to him. He's a brave Fellow, and fcorns to fteal a Victory, or take an Advantage of the Superiority of Numbers. In Savannah, there was not enough of them to give us a Breakfaft. We might have ftarved them in their Works, had not the *Magnanimity* of the Count interpofed in their Favour; and what I have often told you will now be confirmed without a Doubt, that the Englifh are a Parcel of rude, unpolifhed Savages. He, good Man, tho't it ungenerous, with an Army three Times their Number, to cut them to pieces, which he could eafily have done, and therefore led on to the Attack only a fmall Detachment of ours, with a Determination to make them Prifoners of War, (this in Confidence he communicated to Count Dillon and myfelf the Evening before), but the *rudenefs* of thofe Sea-monfters prevented his generous Intentions, having miftook Pity for Cowardice, they had the Infolence to fire on the *Grand Monarque's* Troops before our Maneuvre could be executed. This of courfe was attended with fome Lofs, and as you will readily conceive, occafioned a *little Confufion*, the Americans in their Flight, having (*by Miftake*) fired on their *great and good Allies.* However as the Englifh, by this imprudent Conduct, have forfeited all Title to *Mercy*, they muft expect to pay dearly for their Prefumption, whenever we do them the *Honour* of paying them another Vifit, which I hope will be before long, when I would advife them to make their Wills before they *dare* look us in the Face again, as the Count has fworn to facrifice their *whole Army* to the *Honour and Glory of the French Arms.*

"We are on the Eve of failing again for the Weft Indies, where we fhall continue a few Months. The barren Sands of Georgia being *beneath our Notice*, having indeed found by Experience that they by no Means agree with our Conftitutions.

"The Harmony, my dear Sir, which fubfifted between the *Noble Count and General Lincoln*, was aftonifhing; and if you confider the Satisfaction expreffed in the Conduct of their Officers, Valour of their Troops, and the Showers of Compliments rained down upon them for their Intrepidity, you cannot I am fure, doubt but that the Advantage was on our Side, *notwithftanding the Affair feems to drag after it fome Difagreeables.* It is true we left fome of our Baggage behind, which was not worth bringing off, and which I make no Doubt, thefe poor half ftarved Devils, the *Anglois Georgians*, will be very glad to pick up, when they find *we have left their Coaft clear.*"

[From the New Jerfey Gazette, December 8, 1779.]

Charleftown, October 20.

" THE following are fome of the Reafons that have been affigned, why
the Affault on Savannah did not fucceed,
viz :

" 1ft. The Enemy having a much more
numerous Garrifon than had been repre-
fented; being faid to confift of 1,700 effective Regulars, and a great Number of
Sailors, Marines, Militia and armed Blacks.

" 2d. Their having the Advantage of
the Prefence, Skill, and Activity of fo able
and indefatiguable an Officer as the Hon.
Col. Maitland; who, while our Army was
obliged to wait for the bringing up proper
Cannon and Mortars from the Fleet, (which
took up many Days, and was attended with
inconceivable Difficulties, on Account of
the Diftance of the Shipping, and a Series
of tempeftuous Weather,) was Night and
Day inceffantly engaged in adding to the
Strength and Number of the Works; upon

which it is faid, he employed about 2,000 Negroes.

" 3d. The Enemy having by fome Means or other, difcovered the Approach of our Columns a full Hour before it was poffible for them to reach their refpective Stations; by which they had an Opportunity of pouring upon their Affailants fuch a heavy and inceffant Front, Flank, and Crofs-fire, as no Troops whatever could have fuftained, without being difordered, and occafioned the Order for difcontinuing the Affault, even while the brave French Troops had gained one of the Enemy's Works, and ours, as brave Troops, another.

" Several Frigates having been difpatched from the Count d'Eftaing's Fleet on different Routes, and feveral other very ftriking Circumftances have given Rife to a Conjecture that a ftrong combined Squadron will foon appear in a Quarter where leaft expected. One of the Frigates, it is faid, has been met fteering for Havanna, and another going into Chefapeak Bay."—*Royal Gazette*, Dec. 18.

[From the New Jerfey Gazette, dated November 24, 1779.]

" NOVEMBER 23. Several Ships of Force, belonging to Comte D'Ef-taing's Fleet, arrived in Chefapeak Bay for the Purpofe of landing a few fick and wounded Men, and taking Provifions; this being accomplifhed, they are immediately to proceed for their Station in the Weft Indies."—*Royal Gazette, Dec.* 4.

[From the Royal Gazette, December 18, 1779.]

BY Accounts brought from Chefapeak, we are informed there are in that Bay one French Ship of War of 74, and one of 64 Guns. They had landed about fix hundred Sick, Wounded, and other truly miferable Objects, rendered fuch by the direful Service before Savannah,—their Numbers of Seamen fo much reduced that they could not hand more than one Sail at a Time, and that they had loft feventy Anchors and Cables when off the Coaft of

O

Georgia; that the Comte d'Eftaing was departed for Europe with ten Sail of the Line, feveral of which had loft their Rudders, and were otherwise much *indifpofed*. Several Sail of the Line had returned to the Weft Indies, unable to reach Chefapeak — the Place appointed ˙ for Rendezvous in Cafe of Separation; and it was reported General Scot, one of the Virginian Commanders in the Rebel Service, was killed at the Siege of Savannah.[1]

Journal of the Voyage of His Majefty's Ship Experiment, Commanded by Sir James Wallace.[2]

[From Rivington's Royal Gazette, No. 370, April 15, 1780.]

* * * "SEPTEMBER 24, 1779, fpoke a Cartel from New Providence to Charleftown, with 65 Prifoners on board; Hilton Head, bearing W. N. W. The Car-

---

[1] This proved to be an Error.

[2] This Officer was the Son-in-law of Sir James Wright, the Britifh Governor of Georgia.

tel informed us of having feen 20 Sail
under Hilton Head, and feemingly large
Ships, and ftood to the fouthward; quarter
paft four, the Wind N.W., faw three large
Ships in the S.W. Quarter; wore and
made all the Sail we could from them,
fteering N.E. At 5 found them in Chafe
of us, and faw two Sail to the weftward
bearing down upon us; turned all Hands to
Quarters. At eight, they hoifted French
Colours; and the *Sagitarius* coming very
clofe up with us, fhe brought to, and gave
us two Broadfides. We then drew from
her. But few of her Shot reached us. Got
up a large fore Yard and Sail, and made all
the Sail we could from them. The *Sagitarius* wore, and made Sail after us again.
At half paft eight got within half Gun
Shot. We hoifted our Colors, and came
to Action with her, during which Time all
the other Ships being within Gun Shot of
us, we ftruck our Colours, having neither
Mafts or Sails to command our Ship. The
Ships coming up with us were two *Seventy-*

fours, two Frigates and the Sagitaire of 54
Guns."[1]

[From the Pennſylvania Journal, dated March 1, 1780.]

Baltimore, February 22.

A CORRESPONDENT who arrived in
Town laſt Night from Virginia, hath
been ſo obliging as to communicate the
following Intelligence:

" That an Expreſs from Charleſtown
(South Carolina), reached Peterſburgh[2] the
13th inſtant, with a Diſpatch from Gen.
Lincoln to Gen. Scott, adviſing him THAT
THE ENEMY HAD RECEIVED A
STRONG REINFORCEMENT AT SA-
VANNAH, ſuppoſed to be the Troops
which left New York in December[3] laſt,—
That in Conſequence, Orders were immedi-
ately ſent to Gen. Woodford, to haſten the
March of the Virginia Troops, the laſt of

---

[1] Sir James Wallace was ſent to France for Exchange, there
not being an Officer of equal Rank for Exchange in the Country.

[2] *On Appomattox River*, Virginia.

[3] *The 26th of December.*

whom left Frederickfburgh[1] on Friday laft,
—That Gen. Hogan and his Brigade were
met the 3d inft. ten Miles fouthward of
Halifax, North Carolina,—That the *Fen-
dant*,[2] a French Man-of-War of the Line,
left the Capes the 4th inftant."—*Royal Gazette, March* 8, 1780.

*Burlefque upon an Appeal by Congrefs to the
People of the United States.*

[From Rivington's Royal Gazette, No. 333, Dec. 8, 1779.]

To the Congress,
High and Mighty Fate Fixers.

IN your laft Addrefs to the good People
of America, you roundly afferted, (ra-
ther too precipitately I guefs,) "the Independence of America was fixed as Fate."[3]
The late Difafter in Georgia, and the Suc-

---

[1] *On Rappahanock River*, Virginia.

[2] *Of* 74 *Guns*, Mons. *Vaupreuil* Commander.

[3] The Spirit, but not the Language of this Sentiment is embraced in the Addrefs of Congrefs to the People upon the
Subjeft of the Finances and Public Debt, dated September 13,
1779.

cefs of the Britifh Admiral in the Weft
Indies, make it neceffary again to addrefs
the worthy Yeomen, ieaft they fhould
withhold the neceffary Supplies of Bread
and Pork to your great and good Allies;
but, as I prefume, with d'Eftaing and Lincoln, you are a little chagrined leaft the
Opportunity fhould be loft; I have ven-
tured to indite the following, at the Service
of your High Mightineffes, and am, till
Fate brings on a Reftoration,   Yours,

OLIVER.

*The Addrefs of the Congrefs of the United
States to the Good People, the Farmers.*

WHEN you confider the Bondage you
groaned under, when fubject to the
Britifh Government; we flatter ourfelves
you will not be fo loft to your own Feelings,
and the facred Liberty of your Country,
as to withhold the neceffary Supplies for
our great, good and gallant Allies; who,
"having fought and bled freely in your
Country's Service," are now come amongft

you to eat fparingly and leifurely, of your
Bread and Pork. We affured you in our
former Addrefs, " Your Independence was
fixt as Fate," becaufe founded on your
Virtue, and love of your Country. You
have now a glorious Opportunity of putting
it to the Tryal, and by furnifhing our good
Allies with Provifions, fhewing your difin-
terefted Patriotifm. And as a further Encouragement to the virtuous Yeomen of
thefe States, *We do Refolve*, That the Farmers of thefe States fhall, during the Space
of fix Months, be exempt from all Taxes
whatfoever, on the following Conditions :

That they immediately deliver to Com-
mittees appointed for that Purpofe, all
their Wheat, Flour, Rye and Indian Corn,
together with all the Beef and Pork, re-
ferving for themfelves and Families, all the
Bran, Hufks and Oats, together with the
Offal of the faid Beef and Pork ; and in
order to obviate all Objections to the above
reafonable Requeft, We further ordain, that
the faid Farmers deliver all their Horfes to

the Quarter Mafter General, for the Benefit
of the States, who will furnifh Oats from
the Continental Store, and thereby leave a
fufficient Supply of Oat-meal for the faid
Farmers and their Families : It will be
expected, as the faid Farmers will then
have little Ufe for their Hay and Straw,
they will fend it to the Quarter Mafter
General, with the faid Horfes, to be given
gratis.

And Whereas, it appears to us incon-
fiftent, that any of our fellow Beings
fhould remain in a State of Slavery, whilft
we, for this three Years, laft paft, have
enjoyed the great and glorious Privileges
of Liberty;

We do Refolve, That all Negroes in
Slavery, fhall after the firft Day of January
next, be free from their Mafters, and one
half of them delivered over to his Moft
Chriftian Majefty, the King of France's
Ambaffador, to fatisfy fome urgent Claims,
which we at this Time are not able to
anfwer. The other half of the aforefaid

Negroes, to be hired out to fuch Mafters, as a Committee appointed for that Purpofe fhall approve.

And Whereas, it appears to us, juft and neceffary that the faid Negroes, for the great and valuable Bleffings of Freedom, fhould contribute to the public Expences of thefe States, we further ordain, that the whole of the faid Negroes' Wages be paid into the public Treafury.

And to the GOOD PEOPLE of America in general we DECLARE :

That immediately on the Arrival of Count d'Eftaing at Georgia, we did proclaim a general Day of Thankfgiving, to be held in thefe States, on the ninth Day of December next, not doubting but a complete Victory over all the Britifh Forces in Georgia was "fixt as Fate;" but it has pleafed the Lord, for our fparing the Tories, the Amalekites, and taking only their Sheep and Oxen, their Negroes and Land, to fuffer us to be defeated, and his Moft

P

Chriftian Majefty's Exertions to refcue us from Slavery to prove abortive;

We therefore declare it our Will and Pleafure, that the faid ninth Day of December, be turned into a Day of Fafting and Humiliation, by all thofe who think it moft proper at this Time.

Neverthelefs, anxious not to deprefs the Spirits of the good People of thefe States, we further declare, that all thofe who chufe to make it a Day of Thankfgiving; may with Propriety, thank God it is no worfe.

Eulogy upon Colonel Maitland.

[Lieutenant Colonel John Maitland, of the 71ft Regiment, after fharing the Labors of the Siege, fickened and died of a Fever on the 25th of October, 1779, at Savannah. His Rank as Lieutenant Colonel dated from October 14, 1778. A Letter, dated November 18, 1779, and publifhed in the *Royal Gazette*, December 15th, 1779, fays:]

"THE late Colonel Maitland was one of the moft active Officers at the Commencement, and during the Progrefs of the prefent War. His Zeal and Gallantry were fufficient Incitements to lead him where Danger dignified and rendered a Poft honourable. Though he poffeffed an eafy Fortune, had a Seat in the Houfe of Commons, and was of an advanced Age, yet he never availed himfelf of fuch powerful Pretenfions, or expreffed a Defire of retiring from the Field of Honour. Unfhaken Loyalty, genuine Patriotifm, undaunted Bravery, judicious Conduct, fteady Coolnefs, and unremitting Perfeverance, conftituted his Character as an Officer. His Benevolence was ever exerted when Indigence prefented; he not only relieved, but fympathized with the Diftreffed. To inform him of any Perfon that required charitable Exertion was an ample Recommendation: His Difpofition was fo extremely amiable, that to know him was to admire him. His Addrefs was eafy and engaging; his Language ftrong, nervous and perfuafive. His Affability rendered him pleafing to every Obferver. He was beloved by his Friends, refpected by his Acquaintances, and revered by every Officer and Soldier who had the Happinefs to be under his Command. His Country will feel the Lofs of fo accomplifhed a Chief; his Acquaintances long lament the Lofs of fo valuable a Friend; the Indigent fearch in vain for another fo eminently Benevolent; and the Soldiers, long accuftomed to his pleafing Command, lament his Death, and revere his Memory."

On the Death of Colonel Maitland.

By Mrs. D[elance]y.

[From Rivington's Royal Gazette, No. 373, April 26, 1780.]

O'ER Maitland's Corfe, as Victory reclin'd,
　　Reflecting on the Fate of human Kind;
Is this, (fhe cried), the End of all thy Toils?
What now await thy Laurels, or thy Spoils?
Worn with Fatigue, thou cam'ft thy Friends to fave,
Saw them reliev'd — then funk into the Grave.
Now Grief and Joy together mix their Cries,
Savannah's fav'd — yet gen'rous Maitland dies!
In vain around, thy conqu'ring Soldiers weep,
Thy Eyes are clof'd in Death's eternal Sleep;
Yet while a grateful King and Country fighs,

O'er the lov'd Afhes, Marbles proud, fhall rife ;
Nay, e'en the Foe, releaf'd awhile from Fear,
Confefs thy Virtues and beftow a Tear ;
Own, that as Valour ftrung thy nervous Arm,
To gentle Pity did thy Bofom warm —
Oh ! double Praife to make the Haughty bend,
Yet make a vanquifh't Enemy a Friend ;
Thus Maitland falls — but his undying Name
Shall fhine for ever in the Rolls of Fame.

The SPIRIT of Colonel MAITLAND to Mrs. D——y, on the foregoing Lines.

Elyfian Fields.

FROM thofe bleft Realms where Joys eternal reign,
Accept my Thanks, D——y, for thy Strain.
Within a World, to Malice ever prone,
Where generous Candor is but feldom known,
Where Cenfure's thoufand Tongues unceafing wound,
And private Virtue in the Foe is drown'd ;
'Twas kindly done a Soldier's Name to fave,
Nor let it perifh with him in the Grave.
What, tho' my Country to her Warriors gone,
May grateful raife a monumental Stone,
A few fhort Years their Courfes fhall roll o'er,
And the vain Structure will exift no more;
But far beyond whate'er a Nation pays,
My Soul efteems the fair D——y's Praife.
Where's now the haughty Heav'n afpiring Tomb,
Rear'd for her Cæfar, by afflicted Rome?
Fall'n beneath the ruthlefs Hand of Age !
Yet Cæfar lives in Maro's facred Page !

So when in Ruin lies the laurel'd Buft,
And Tombs and Statues moulder in the Duft,
Thy Verfe, D——y, fhall tranfmit to Fame
Immortal as your own, your Maitland's Name.

Epitaph on the Honourable Colonel Maitland.

[From Rivington's Royal Gazette, No. 401, Aug. 2, 1780.]

WHEN Gallic Perfidy and Rebel Pride,
    Prefumed the Britifh Lion to fubdue,
With rapid Wing, but not before untried,
    From Beaufort's Banks the gallant Maitland flew.

In Time to fave, he reached Savannah's Coaft,
    The Force of France, and perjured Foes defied;
Repell'd, difperf'd the formidable Hoft,
    Preferv'd a Country, blefs'd the Day, and DIED.

Opening of Trade with Georgia.

[From Rivington's Royal Gazette, No. 383, May 31, 1780.]

Dublin, March 14.

THIS Day at Noon, the Lord Mayor received two Letters from the Commiffioners of his Majefty's Revenue, of which the following are Copies:

My LORD.

I am commanded by the Commiſſioners of his Majeſty's Revenue to tranſmit to your Lordſhip, for the Information of the Merchants and Traders of this City, the incloſed Copy of a Letter which the Board have this Day received from John Robinſon, Eſqr., Secretary to the Right Honourable the Lords Commiſſioners of his Majeſty's Treaſury, from which it appears, that the Province of Georgia is declared to be in the Peace of his Majeſty.

I have the Honour to be, my Lord, your Lordſhip's moſt humble Servant,

W. MOLESWORTH.

Cuſtom Houſe, Dublin, March 14, 1780.
Rt. Hon. Lord Mayor.

My LORDS and GENTLEMEN.

HAVING laid before the Lords Commiſſioners of his Majeſty's Treaſury a Letter from Lord George Germain, dated the 11th of February laft, tranfmitting the Copy of a Proclamation which has been publifhed in Georgia, declaring that Province in the Peace of his Majefty, and defiring my Lord will give the neceffary Directions to the Officers of the Revenue throughout his Majefty's Dominions, to permit the fame Trade and Intercourfe with Georgia as might lawfully be carried on before the Act of 15th of his prefent Majefty, unlefs where Alterations have been made by fubfequent Acts. I am commanded by their Lordfhips to direct you to give the neceffary Orders to your Officers accordingly.

I am, my Lords and Gentlemen, your moft humble Servant,

JOHN ROBINSON.

Treafury Chambers, March 8, 1780.
Com'rs Revenue, Ireland.

Letter with Criticifms upon the Siege of Savannah.

[From Rivington's Royal Gazette, No. 428, Nov. 4, 1780.]

To WILLIAM LIVINGSTON, Efq.[1]

Metiri fe quemque fuo Modulo ac Pede. verum eft. HOR.[2]

I HAVE the Pleafure, which I wifh always to enjoy, of being a Stranger to your Perfon. But who is a Stranger to your Character? And what Character but yours could meanly fkulk under Secuiity, to profane the moft honored Names — to exult on the Fate of a patriot Martyr,[3] — and, and with malignant Breath, attempt to blaft thofe Laurels, which will bloom when Livingfton is plunged among his kindred Fiends?

Having had Patience enough to perufe an Addrefs in Loudon's New York *Cafket,*[4]

---

[1] An ardent Patriot, and Governor of New Jerfey.

[2] It is a Truth, that every one ought to meafure himfelf by his own proper Foot and Standard.—Smart's *Horace,* Epiftle vii.

[3] Major Andre.

[4] Publifhed at Fifhkill, N Y., at this Period.

Q

figned Z, and faid to come from you, I
cannot refift the benevolent Impulfe, of
warning thofe who may unwarily take the
fame Rubbifh, of the burning Embers it
conceals.   In attacking you with your
own Weapon, the Pen, I do not undertake
to convince you ; whoever points out the
right Road, fhews the Way your Nature
will not permit you to purfue.   Tho' the
envenomed Shafts of Malice cannot penetrate your Armor of confcious Vice, fhall
Malice bend her bow with Impunity?
Forbid it Juftice!   Forbid it, ye generous
Feelings of Humanity!

You meafure all great and good Actions
by the Standard of a perverfe Mind, and
cannot look for their Source, but in a black
and vifcious Heart, like Livingfton's.   Ma-
levolence ever cafts a difmal Shade over
the fineft Pictures.   In the Language of
your poifonous Tongue, you will defcribe
Brutus as a *mere* Affafin,—Cæfar as going
to the Senate on the Ides of March, with

a *torpid Mind,*—and Cato as dying with *all his native Sullennefs.*

Callous to all the amiable Senfation which dignify human Nature, is it poffible for you to conceive why wife Men have deemed the greateft of all Victories to be, a Victory over the Paffions? When I reflect on a fignal Victory of this Kind, I feel myfelf compelled to turn from fo loathfome an Object as you are, and exclaim with Shakefpeare's Prince,

———————— Thou haft been,
As one, in fuffering all, haft fuffered nothing ;
Give me the Man
That is not Paffion's Slave, and I will wear him
In my Heart's Core, ay, in my Heart of Hearts.[1]

[1] " Since my dear Soul was Miftrefs of her Choice,
  And could of Men diftinguifh, her election
  Hath feal'd thee for herfelf: for thou haft been
  As one, in fuffering all, that fuffers nothing;
  A Man, that Fortune's buffets and rewards
  Haft ta'en with equal Thanks : and bleff'd are thofe,
  Whofe Blood and Judgment are fo well co-mingled,
  That they are not a Pipe for Fortune's Finger
  To found what Stop fhe pleafe.   Give me that **Man**
  That is not Paffion's Slave, and I will wear him
  In my Heart's Core, ay, in my Heart of Heart,
  As I do thee."—*Hamlet,* Act iii, Scene ii.

It is ftrange fo fhrewd a Politician as Mr. Livingfton *thinks himfelf*, fhould exceed the Limits of his Abilities, in difplaying his deep Difcoveries to the gaping Throng. As you have turn'd Soldier *only*, in your Clofet, 'twas fomewhat bold to decide fo peremptorily on Deeds of War. Accordingly, like an inexperienced General, you have expofed your weak Side to the Enemy, and rafhly attacked him where he is invulnerable. Whether your Defcription of Charleftown[1] is your own Offfpring, or the Tale of one of the trembling Garrifon, who view'd it thro' the falfe Medium of his Fears, it is equally immaterial; its *Falfehood* is notorious to Thoufands of brave Witneffes, and its improbability obvious to every military Profeffor.

When the *invincible* Troops of your *great* and *good* Ally, fupported by your renowned *Continental Army* appeared before Savannah,

---

[1] Alluding to the Capture of Charlefton, which occurred May 12, 1780.

it was judged imprudent to *affault* an almoft unfortified Poft, thinly garrifoned, very moderately furnifhed with Artillery, much extended, and deftitute of a fuperior naval Force. When a Body of Britifh Troops, not proportionally fuperior to the Numbers of the Garrifon, fhew themfelves before Charleftown, Mr. Livingfton, *at his warning Defk*, votes for the *Affault;* by which he, unawares, pays them the higheft Compliment. The Place was provided with a Profufion of Artillery, and every kind of military Stores.

No Place or Fortrefs can have greater natural Advantages than Charleftown. Towards Afhley River, the only adjoining Water at firft in the Power of the Affailants, there is one acceffible Landing. This the befieged had cautioufly fortified in Front, and could have protected by a heavy interfecting Fire from various Batteries.

On the Land Side, the Defences you ignominioufly term *Intrenchments*, would have been lefs formidable, had they been compofed of more permanent Materials. Count d'Eftaing tired himfelf in trying to *battre en bréche* againft the *Sand* Banks of Savannah. From the Days of Goliah to thofe of Livingfton, there never were Troops who could not call a Halt at a wide Ditch nine Feet deep, two Rows of Pallifades in its Bottom, and flanked with Cannon.

Thefe confumate Generals, the Count d'Eftaing and General Lincoln, after having long remained "before fuch a Place" as Savannah, "with open Trenches, and all the Apparel of a regular Siege," tried an *Affault*. They attempted to carry by Storm a fquare Redoubt, confifting fimply of a Ditch and Sand Parapet, without a Pallifade or Fraife on it! The vaunting *Grenadiers de France Sabre a la Main*, took French Leave by a precipitate Flight, leaving Heaps of their martial Comrades in the Ditch, and immortal GLORY WITH THE GARRISON.

General Lincoln's *Sanctum Sanctorum*, the horn Work, clofed in the Gorge, and furnifhed with the heavieft Cannon, juftly

claims the Title of a Fort. Beyond the intricate Line, no Obſtruction was omitted, and the ſecond Ditch was enfiladed by the Cannon˙of the Outworks.[1] * * * *
The Eſplanade extended near a Mile; in which Space not a Houſe, Tree or even Poſt was left ſtanding. The Flatneſs of the Ground made this Eſplanade very advantageous to the Beſieged; while the impaſſable Marſhes from each River, forming a Kind of Iſthmus at every two hundred Yards, under the Line of five of their braveſt Batteries, made it impoſſible to approach, otherwiſe than by the judicious Reſource adopted.

Whoever reflects on the aſtoniſhing Cannonade maintained for ſo long a Time, by the Garriſon of Charleſton, and compares it with the Loſs of its Enemy, will beſtow no great Share of *Glory* on the Former, for betraying Terror in a random and ill directed Fire; ſurely no *Soldier* can withhold

---

[1] The Subject here changes from Savannah to Charleſton.

due Praife from the Latter, for having
gained the glorious Prize at fo fmall an
Expenfe.   Little more Labour would have
made a Variety of practicable Breaches in
the Works, and CHARLESTON would have
felt the Fury of incenfed Brittons.   The
frightened Garrifon knew it, and obtained
what they folicited — not *Glory*, but MER-
CY — a celeftial Virtue, and of courfe un-
known to LIVINGSTON.

A SOLDIER.

Advertifement.

[From Rivington's Royal Gazette, No. 333, Dec. 8, 1779.]

THE gallant and intrepid Conduct of
the brave GARRISON at SAVAN-
NAH demanding the warmeft Acknow-
ledgment from every loyal Breaft, it is
propofed to raife a Fund for the Purpofe of
relieving the Sick, Wounded, and Families
of thofe who have fallen ; as well as to give
fuch Affiftance to the Soldiers, as Circumftances will admit.   A Subfcription for

thefe Purpofes is now refpectfully offered; the Money to be difpofed of agreeable to the Opinion of a general Meeting of the Subfcribers, with the Approbation of his Excellency the Commander-in-Chief. In the Mean-time a Committee of fixteen is appointed to collect Subfcriptions.

N. B. Donations will be received by Mr. Rivington and Mr. Gaine.

Charleftown, S. Carolina, October 26.

LAST Thurfday Evening, [October 21ft, 1779,] the Hon. Major General Lincoln, commanding the Troops in the Southern Department, returned here from the fouthward.—*Quoted in the Royal Gazette December* 29, 1779.

R

APPENDIX.

CORRESPONDENCE BETWEEN COUNT D'ES-
TAING AND GENERAL PREVOST.

Continued from Page 94.

*Reply of Major General Prevoſt to the Sum-
mons of Count D'Eſtaing.*

Savannah, September 16, 1779.

Sir,

I AM juſt now honored with your Excellency's
Letter of this Date, containing a Summons
for me to furrender this Town to the Arms
of his Majeſty the King of France; which I
had juſt delayed to anſwer till I had ſhown it to
the King's civil Governor.

I hope your Excellency will have a better
Opinion of me, and of Britiſh Troops, than to
think either will furrender on general Summons,
without any ſpecific Terms.

If you, Sir, have any to propofe, that may

with honour be accepted of by me, you can mention them, both with regard to Civil and Military; and I will then give my Anfwer. In the mean Time I will promife, upon my Honour, that nothing with my Confent or Knowledge, fhall be deftroyed in either this Town or River.

A. Prevost.

His Excellency, Count D'Eftaing, Commanding the French Forces, &c. &c.

Letter from Count D'Eftaing to General Prevoft.

Camp before Savannah, Sept. 16th, 1779.

Sir,

I HAVE juft received your Excellency's Anfwer to the Letter I had the Honour of writing to you this Morning. You are fenfible that it is the Part of the Befieged to propofe fuch Terms as they may defire; and you cannot doubt of the Satisfaction I fhall have in confenting to thofe which I can accept confiftently with my duty.

I am informed that you continue intrenching yourfelf. It is a Matter of very little Importance to me; however for Form's fake, I muft defire that you will defift during our Conferences.

The different Columns which I had ordered to ftop, will continue their March, but without approaching your Pofts, or reconnoitering your Situation.

I have the Honour to be, with Refpect,
  Sir, your Excellency's moft humble
   and moft obedient Servant,
     Estaing.

His Excellency, General Prevoft, Major General in the Service of his Britannic Majefty, and Commander in Chief at Savannah, in Georgia.

P. S. I appraife your Excellency that I have not been able to refufe the Army of the United States, uniting itfelf with that of the King.

The Junction will probably be effected this Day. If I have not an Anfwer therefore immediately, you muft confer in future with General Lincoln and me.

Reply of General Prevoſt.

Savannah, September 16, 1779.

Sir,

I AM honored with your Excellency's Letter in reply to mine of this Day.

The Buſineſs we have had in Hand being of importance, there being various Intereſts to diſcuſs, a juſt Time is abſolutely neceſſary to deliberate. I am therefore to propoſe that a Ceſſation of Hoſtilities ſhall take place for twenty-four Hours from this Date; and to requeſt that your Excellency will order your Columns to fall back to a greater Diſtance, and out of Sight of our Works, or I ſhall think myſelf under the Neceſſity to direct their being fired upon. If they did not reconnoitre any Thing this Afternoon, they were ſure within the Diſtance.

I have the Honour to be, &c.,

A. Prevost.

His Excellency Count D'Eſtaing, &c., &c.

*Letter from Count D'Eſtaing to General
Prevoſt.*

Camp before Savannah, Sept. 16, 1779.
Sir,

I CONSENT to the Truce you aſk. I ſhall
continue till the Signal for Retreat To-
morrow Night, the 17th, which will ſerve alſo
to announce the Recommencement of Hoſtilities. It is unneceſſary to obſerve to your Excellency, that this Suſpenſion of Arms is entirely
in your Favour, ſince I cannot be certain that
you will not make uſe of it to fortify yourſelf,
at the ſame Time that the Propoſitions you
ſhall make may be inadmiſſible.

I muſt obſerve to you alſo, how important it
is, that you ſhould be fully aware of your own
Situation as well as that of the Troops under
your Command. Be aſſured that I am tho-
roughly acquainted with it. Your Knowledge
in military Affairs will not ſuffer you to be
ignorant, that a due Examination of that Cir-
cumſtance always precedes the March of the Columns ; and that this Preliminary is not carried
into Execution by the mere Show of Troops.

I have ordered them to withdraw before
Night comes on, to prevent any Cauſe of Com-

plaint on your Part. I underftand that my Civility in this Refpect has been the Occafion, that the Chevalier de Chambis, a Lieutenant in the Navy, has been made a Prifoner of War.

I propofe fending out fome fmall advanced Pofts to-morrow Morning. They will place themfelves in fuch a Situation as to have in View the four Entrances into the Wood in order to prevent a fimilar Miftake in Future. I do not know whether two Columns, commanded by the Vifcount de Noailles and the Count de Dillon,[1] have fhown too much Ardour,

---

[1] "Count Arthur Dillon was the Son of Henry, the Eleventh Vifcount Dillon, in the Peerage of Ireland. His Father was a Colonel in the French Service. His Grandfather, Arthur, went into the Army of France, and commanded an Irifh Regiment after his Father. * * * The Grandfather of Count Dillon was, in 1705, made Marfhal of the Camp, and Governor of Toulon; and fubfequently a Lieutenant-General of France. Dillon's Regiment was commanded, after the Death of Marfhal Dillon, by his Son James, a Knight of Malta; and when he fell at the Head of this Regiment at Fontenoy, his Brother Edward fucceeded to his Command; and it was this Regiment which the young Count Arthur led into the Action at the Siege of Savannah. He was involved in the Troubles of the French Revolution, and fuffered under the Guillotine in 1794. His Daughter Fanny was married to Count Bertrand, and was diftinguifhed by her Fidelity to the Emperor, during his long Imprifonment at St. Helena."— Stevens's *Hift. of Georgia*, ii, 226.

or whether your Cannoniers have not paid a proper Refpect to the Truce fubfifting between us; but this I know, that what has happened this Night is a Proof that Matters will foon come to a Decifion between us one Way or another.

I have the Honour to be, &c.,

ESTAING.

His Excellency, General Prevoft, Major General in the Service of his Britannic Majefty, and Commander in Chief at Savannah, in Georgia.

Reply to the foregoing Letter.

Savannah, September 17, 1779.

Sir,

IN Anfwer to the Letter of your Excellency, which I had the Honour to receive about twelve laft Night, I am to acquaint you, that having laid the whole Correfpondence before the King's civil Governor, and the military Officers of Rank, affembled in Council of War, the unanimous Determination has been that though we cannot look upon our Poft as abfolutely impregnable, yet that it may and ought

S

to be defended; therefore, the evening Gun to be fired this Evening at an Hour before Sundown, ſhall be the Signal for recommencing Hoſtilities, agreeable to your Excellency's Propoſal.

I have the Honour to be, &c.,

A. PREVOST.

[White's *Hiſt. Georgia*, P. 349.]

Engliſh Account of the Capture of Savannah.

[From the London Gazette, December 21, 1779.]

Admiralty Office, December 21.

CAPTAIN Chriſtian, of his Majeſty's armed Ship, the *Vigilant*, arrived here early this Morning, with a Letter from Captain Henry,[1] of his Majeſty's Ship *Fowey*, to Mr. Stephens, of which the following is an Extract:

Savannah River, Georgia, Nov. 8, 1779.

I beg you will be pleaſed to communicate to the Right Honourable my Lords Commiſſion-

---

[1] Captain John Henry was born in Angleſea, Sept. 28, 1731, entered the Navy in 1744, was a Lieutenant in 1762, and became Poſt Captain Nov. 22, 1777. He became Rear Admiral July 4, 1794, Vice Admiral Feb. 14, 1799, and Admiral April 23, 1804.—Marſhall's *Royal Naval Biography*, i, 64.

ers of the Admiralty the following important Particulars:

That the French Fleet, under the Count D'Eftaing, confifting of twenty Sail of the Line, two of fifty Guns, and eleven Frigates, arrived on this Coaft the 1ft of September paft, from Cape François, having on board a large Body of Troops, purpofely for the Reduction of this Province. They failed from the Cape on the 20th of Auguft, and came through the windward Paffage, when they difpatched two Ships of the Line and three Frigates to Charleftown, to announce their coming, and prepare the rebel Force by Sea and Land to join the Count D'Eftaing. Thefe two Ships of the Line and Frigates, were feen from Tybee, the 3d of September, when Lieutenant Lock, of the *Rofe*, was fent to reconnoitre them, and brought Word they were French.

Lieutenant Whitworth, who commands the *Keppel* armed Brig, was ordered to get ready a faft failing Tender of his own, to proceed to New York with this Intelligence, and failed with his Difpatches on the 6th, but was chafed in again by feven Sail. On the 7th, at Night, he made another Attempt, wherein there is every Reafon to hope he was fuccefsful.

On the 8th, forty-one Sail were difcovered to the Southward of Tybee, plying to the Windward. The Wind being Northerly, as it had been for fome Days paſt, drove them to the Southward of this Port.

Major General Prevoſt, at Savannah, was immediately acquainted with their Appearance, who went to work with every Exertion to increaſe the Fortifications of the Town. Deſpatches were ſent to the Hon. Colonel Maitland, who was poſted with Part of the Army on Port Royal Iſland, and to Captain Chriſtian, of his Majeſty's Ship *Vigilant*, to repair to Savannah as foon as poſſible, with the Troops, Ships and Galleys there.

The *Fowey*, *Roſe*, *Keppel*, armed Brig, and *Germain;* provincial armed Ship, were ſo placed that if the French Ships came in ſuperior, we might run up the River; and the leading Marks for the Bar were cut down.

On the 9th, the whole French Fleet anchored off the Bar, and next Day four Frigates weighed and came to Tybee Anchorage. It was determined on their Approach, to run up the River with the King's Ships, and join our Force with the General for the Defence of the Town. At this Time the French were ſending Troops from their Ships, which were firſt put into ſmall Crafts from Charleſtown, and run into Oſabaw Inlet; from whence they were landed in Launches at Bowley, thirteen Miles from Savannah, under Cover of four Galleys; and their Frigates were preparing to advance up the River.

From the 10th to the 13th we were buſy ſending to Town, Part of the *Fowey* and *Roſe's* Guns and Ammunition, in Veſſels ſent by the General for that Purpoſe. On the 13th the *Fowey* and *Roſe*, being much lightened, ſailed over the Mud Flat to Five-Fathom-Hole, three Miles below the Town, from whence was ſent up the Remainder of the Guns and Ammunition.

The *Comet* Galley and *Keppel* armed Brig were directed to place themſelves below the Mud Flat, ſo as to cover the Paſſage of Colonel Maitland, with the King's Troops from Port Royal, through Wall's Cut, from whom we had not heard ſince the Communication by Boats being cut off.

The 14th and 15th the Seamen were employed in landing the Cannon and Ammunition of the Ships from the ſmall Veſſels; and this having been done, the Seamen were appointed to the different Batteries, and the Marines incorporated with the Grenadiers of the 60th Regiment.

On the 16th, the Count D'Eftaing fummoned the General to furrender the Town to the Arms of his moft Chriftian Majefty;[1] at the fame Time faying, his Troops were the fame who fo recently ftormed and conquered the Grenadas; that their Courage and prefent Ardour were fo great, that any Works we fhould raife, or any Oppofition we could make, would be of no Import. Not intimidated with this Language, the General called a Meeting of Field and Sea Officers, when it was refolved to take twenty-four Hours to confider. In that Time the Troops from Beaufort arrived in Boats from the *Vigilant* and Tranfports (in Callibogie Sound), through Wall's Cut, under the Direction of Lieutenant Goldenfborough of the *Vigilant;* and now the Count D'Eftaing had his final Anfwer, "that we were unanimoufly determined to defend the Town."

[1] This Summons, in the Name of D'Eftaing alone, for a Surrender to the Arms of France, led Gen. Lincoln, upon his arrival, to remonftrate to the Count, as the Americans were acting in conjunction with him. The Matter was foon fettled, and it was agreed that all Negotiations fhould in Future be conducted jointly with him.—Bowen's *Lincoln*, 302.

The General, ever attentive to increaſe the
Defences of the Town, with Captain Moncrief,
our principal Engineer, was now indefatigably,
Night and Day, raiſing new Works and Batteries, which aſtoniſhed our Enemies; and every
Officer, Soldier and Sailor worked with the
utmoſt Cheerfulneſs; and I have the Pleaſure
to inform their Lordſhips, the General has been
pleaſed to expreſs his particular Satisfaction with
the Services of the Officers of the King's Ships
and Tranſports during the whole Siege.

It being apprehended that the Enemy's Ships
might come too near the Town, and annoy the
Rear of our Lines, it was judged expedient to
ſink a Number of Veſſels to ſtop the Paſſage.
His Majeſty's Ship *Roſe*, making at this Time
ſeventeen Inches of Water an Hour, after
ſheathing her as low as we could at Cockſpur,
her Bottom Worm-eaten quite through, and
her Stern rotten, as appears by a Survey of
Shipwrights held on her a ſhort Time before,
wherein it was declared ſhe could not ſwim over
two Months, her Guns, Men, and Ammunition
being on Shore, I thought her the moſt eligible
to Sink, as her Weight would keep her acroſs
the Channel, when lighter Veſſels could not,

owing to the Rapidity of the Current, and hard fandy Bottom, which prevented them from fticking faft when they were funk. The *Savannah* armed Ship, purchafed into the King's Service fome Time before by Commodore Sir James Wallace, was fcuttled and funk alfo; four Tranfports were funk befides, which blocked up the Channel; feveral fmaller Veffels were funk above the Town, and a Boom laid acrofs the River, to prevent the Enemy fending down fire Rafts among our Shipping, or landing Troops in our Rear.

The *Fowey*, *Keppel* Brig, *Comet* Galley, and *Germain* provincial armed Ship, were got to Town previous to finking the Veffels; the *Germain* having her Guns in, was placed off Yamacraw to flank our Lines.[1]

Three French Frigates were now advanced up the River to the Mud Flat; one of them having 12-Pounders, with two Rebel Galleys, carrying two 18-Pounders in their Prows, anchored in Five-Fathom-Hole; from whence

[1] The *Germain*, the only Veffel that was not difmantled, was anchored above the Town, and commanded every Approach through the low Grounds bordering the Mufgrove Creek.—Stevens's *Hift. Georgia*, ii, 215.

the Frigate failed into the Back River, with the intent to cannonade the Rear of our Lines. They threw a great Number of Shot, which, being at their utmoft Range, did no Execution. The Galleys, advancing nearer, did fome Damage to the Houfes. A few Shot now and then from the River Battery made them keep a refpectable Diftance.

The French having now made regular Approaches, and finifhed their Batteries of Mortars and Cannon, near enough to our Works, on the 3d of October, at Midnight, opened their Bomb Battery of nine large Mortars. At Daybreak they alfo opened with thirty-feven Pieces of heavy Cannon, landed from their Fleet, and fired on our Lines and Batteries with great Fury.

This lafted Day and Night till the Morning of the 9th, when finding little Notice taken of their Shot and Shells, at Daybreak ftormed with their whole Force, the Count D'Eftaing at their Head.

This Attempt proved moft fatal to them, for they met with fo very fevere a Repulfe from only three hundred Men, affifted by the Grape-fhot from the Batteries, that from this Day

T

they worked with indefatiguable Labour to carry off their Cannon and Mortars, and defcended to a Degree of Civility we had hitherto been Strangers to. Their Lofs was very great; moft of their beft Officers and Soldiers being killed or wounded, the Count D'Eftaing among the Latter.

On the Night of the 17th, the French entirely quitted their Works, retreated to their Boats, and embarked under Cover of their Galleys. General Lincoln, with the Rebel Army, retreated up the Country with the greateft Precipitation, burning every Bridge behind them; and we are told their Army is totally difperfed.

The French have been favoured by the Weather to their utmoft Wifhes the whole Time of their being on this Coaft; their great Ships lying conftantly at Anchor in fourteen Fathoms, and the fmall Craft from Charleftown employed watering them from this River. The only Accident we know they met with, was lofing one Boat with one hundred Men.

When the French Troops were all embarked, an Officer was fent on Shore to exchange Prifoners. This being finifhed, they loft no

Time in venturing down the River with their Frigates and Galleys to Tybee.

The *Vigilant*, with the *Scourge* and *Vindictive* Galleys, the *Snake*, half Galley, and three Tranfports, were obliged to remain at Callibogie the whole Siege, where Captain Chriftian, of the *Vigilant*, fecured them in fo ftrong a Pofition, and erected a Battery on Shore to protect them, that the French and Rebels thought it moft prudent to let them alone. They are now all at Tybee, the French Fleet having left this Coaft the 26th of October; and their Frigates left this River the 2d of November.

On the 4th of November the *Myrtle*, Navy Victualler, who was taken by the French, and turned into a watering Veffel, being blown out of this River a few Days before they left it, returned to Tybee with a Rebel Galley, expecting to find their Friends. They both fell into our Hands. The Galley is called the *Rutledge*, carries two 18-Pounders in her Prow, and four Sixes in her Waift. I have named her the *Viper*, and appointed Mr. John Steel, Mafter's Mate of the *Rofe*, to command her, with an Eftablifhment fimilar to other Galleys, until the Admiral's Pleafure is known. Mr. Steel's Behaviour at the Battery, on the Spot where the French and Rebels ſtormed our Line, deſerves particular Notice.

His Majeſty's Ship *Ariel* of twenty-four Guns, on a Cruiſe from Charleſtown (when the French came on this Coaſt), was taken on the 11th of September, after a gallant Reſiſtance, by the French Frigate *Amazon,* of thirty-ſix Guns. His Majeſty's Ship *Experiment* having loſt all her Maſts and Bowſprit in a Gale of Wind on her Paſſage from New York to Savannah, fell into the Middle of the French Fleet off this Bar, and was taken on the 24th of September, together with the *Myrtle,* Navy Victualler, and *Champion,* Store Ship.

LIST OF THE FRENCH FLEET ON THIS COAST UNDER COUNT D'ESTAING.

Firſt Diviſion — Mr. Bougainville.

Le Guerriere, -	-	74	Le Province, -	- 64
Le Magnifique,	-	74	Le Marſeilles,	- 64
Le Cæſar,	-	- 74	Le Fantaſque,	- 64
Le Vengeur,	-	74		

Second Diviſion — Comte D'Eſtaing.

Le Languedoc,	-	74	Le Vaillant, -	- 74
Le Robuſte,	-	74	Le Artizien,	- 64
Le Zele,	-	- 74	Le Sagitaire, -	- 54
Le Annibal,	-	74		

Third Divifion.

Le Tonant, -	- 80	Le Pendant, -	- 74
Le Diademe,	- 74	Le Refleche,	- 64
Le Hector, -	- 74	Le Sphynx, -	- 64
Le Dauphine Royal,	70	Le Roderique, Store-	
Le Royal, -	- 70	fhip, -	- 00

Frigates.

Le Fortune, -	- 38	La Chimere, -	- 36
L'Amazon,	- 36	La Bordeaux,	- 36
L'Iphigene, -	- 36	La Bricoli, -	- 36
La Blanche,	- 36	La Lys, -	- 18

Englifh Ships Taken.

Experiment, -	- 50	Lively, -	- 20
Ceres,	- 18	Alert Cutter,	- 14

The Land Forces on board this Fleet were the Irifh Brigade (Dillon), the Regiment of Foix, the Grenadiers, Light Infantry, and a Picquet of the Regiments of Armagnac, Agenois, Bram, and Royal Roufillon, and of the Colony Troops of Guadaloupe, Martinique, Cape François, and Port au Prince, with Marines of the Ships, amounted to about five Thoufand five Hundred Men. They landed at firft four Thoufand, and at different Landings about three Hundred more (the Rebels had three Thoufand), befides fome Hundreds of free Blacks and Mulattoes, taken on board in the Weſt Indies.

This Fleet is very badly manned, very ſickly, and the Ships in very bad Condition,—ſhort of Anchors and Cables, having no running Rigging to reel but what came out of the *Champion* Store Ship, from New York, and intended for this Port. We have every Reaſon to believe this Expedition coſt them two Thouſand Men.

RETURN OF SEAMEN AND MARINES KILLED AND WOUNDED DURING THE SIEGE.

Fowey—One Marine killed, one wounded.

RETURN OF THE OFFICERS OF THE AMERICAN FORCES WHO WERE KILLED AND WOUNDED IN THE ACTION AT SAVANNAH, OCT. 9, 1779.

Killed.

Second Regiment—Major Wiſe, Lieutenant Bailey.

General Williamſon's Brigade—Captain Beraud.

Charleſtown Regiment—Captain Shepherd.

South Carolina Artillery—Captain Lieutenant Donnom.

Major Jones, Aid to General McIntoſh.

Wounded.

Cavalry—Brigadier-General Count Pulaſki, Captain Bendelo, Captain Giles.

Second Regiment—Captain Roux, Lieutenants Gray and Petre.

Third Regiment—Captain Tanar, Lieutenants Gaſton and Deſſaufure.

Sixth Regiment—Captain Bowie.

Virginia Levies—Lieutenants Parker and Walker.

Light Infantry—Capt. Smith, of the Third; Captains Warren and Hogin, of the Fifth; Lieutenant Vleland, of the Second; Lieutenant Parſons of the Fifth.

South Carolina Militia—Capt. Davis, Lieutenants Bruneau, Wilkie and Wardel.

Engliſh Return of Caſualties in the different Corps during the Siege.

[From White's Hiſtory of Georgia, P. 352.]

ONE Captain, 2 Lieutenants, 1 Enſign, 4 Sergeants, 32 Rank and File, killed; 2 Captains, 2 Lieutenants, 2 Sergants, 1 Drummer, 56 Rank and File, wounded; 2 Drummers, 2 Rank and File, miſſing; 5 Sergeants, 2 Drummers, 41 Rank and File Deſerted.

Names of Officers Killed.

Lieutenant Henry McPherſon, 1ſt Battalion 71ſt, 24th September.

Lieutenant Tawſe,[1] of ditto, and Captain-Lieutenant of Dragoons, 9th of October.

Captain Simpſon, Georgia Loyaliſt, 8th of October.

Enſign Pollard, 2d Battalion, De Lancey's, 4th of ditto.

Names of Officers·Killed.

Captain Cozens, 3d Battalion New Jerſey Volunteers, 24th of September.

Lieutenant Smollet Campbell, 2d Battalion 71ſt, and Lieutenant of Dragoons, 9th of October.

Captain Henry, of the South Carolina Royaliſts, 9th of October.

A. PREVOST, M. G.

Camp Savannah, Oct. 18, 1779.

---

[1] Thomas Tawſe; Date of Rank as Lieutenant, December 6, 1775.

Letter from General Lincoln to Congrefs.
" *Charlefton, October* 22, 1779.
Sir,

IN my Laft, of the 5th ult., I had the Honor
of informing Congrefs that Count d'Eftaing
was arrived off Savannah.[1]

1 SECRET PROCEEDINGS IN CONGRESS. September 26, 1779.—
" The Prefident laid before Congrefs two Letters which he had
received from Mr. Gerard, written to him by J. Plombard, and
dated Charlefton, South Carolina, one the 5th and the other the
8th September inftant, which were read, giving Information of
the Arrival of Count d'Eftaing at Georgia: Whereupon,

" *Refolved*, That Copies of the Letters from Mr. Plombard
to Mr. Gerard, of the 5th and 8th of September, inftant, communicated by Mr. Gerard to the Prefident, be fent to General
Wafhington. That the General be alfo informed of the Inten-
tion of our Ally, that the Armament under Count d'Eftaing
fhall operate againft the Enemy in thefe United States; and that
General Wafhington be authorized and directed to concert and
execute fuch Plans of Coöperation with the Minifter of France,
or the Count, as he may think Proper.

" *Whereas*, Congrefs have received authentick Information of
the Arrival of Count d'Eftaing with a powerful Fleet to coöperate with thefe United States; and whereas, by the vigorous
Exertions of the faid States, the allied Forces may be enabled
to ftrike an important Blow againft the Enemy,

" *Refolved*, That it be moft earneftly recommended to the
feveral States to furnifh General Wafhington with fuch Aid as he

V

Orders were immediately given for affembling the Troops. They reached Zubly's Ferry and its Vicinity on the 11th, and fome were thrown over. The 12th and 13th were fpent in croffing the Troops and Baggage, which was effected, though not without great Fatigue, from the Want of Boats,[1] and badnefs of the Roads through a deep Swamp of near three Miles, in which are many large Creeks. The Bridges over them the Enemy had broken down. We encamped upon the Heights of Ebenezer, twenty-three Miles from Savannah, and were joined by Troops from Augufta under General

may require of them refpectively, as well by Detachments from their Militia as by providing that the allied Armaments in the United States be fpeedily and effectually furnifhed with ample Supplies of Bread and other Provifions; and that the moft vigorous Exertions be made for that Purpofe."— *Secret Journals of Congrefs,* i, 127.

[1] The only Conveniences for croffing were two Canoes, one of which would hold three, and the other fifteen Men, and an unfinifhed Flat. Lincoln ordered this to be completed, and a Raft to be made of the Boards and Timber of the Buildings. The next Day, the Army began to crofs, and the Raft fank on its firft Trial; but another Canoe was obtained, and with the aid of this and of the now finifhed Flat, moft of the Troops were tranfported to the Georgia Side before Night.—Bowen's *Life of Lincoln,* 301.

McIntofh. The 14th, not being able to afcertain whether the Count had yet landed his Troops, though feveral Expreffes had been fent for that Purpofe, we remained encamped. On the 15th, being advifed that the Count had embarked Part of his Troops, that he would that Night take Poft nine Miles from Savannah, we moved, and encamped at Cherokee Hill, nine Miles from the Town. The 16th, we formed a Junction before Savannah. After reconnoitering the Enemy's Works, and finding the Town well covered, and knowing their Determination to defend it, it was deemed neceffary to make fome Approaches, and try the Effects of Artillery[1] From the 18th to the 23d, we

---

[1] " While the Siege was going on, detached Parties of the Americans obtained fome Succefs againft a few Troops of the Enemy, who had not fucceeded in getting into Savannah before the Town was completely invefted. On the 19th, Pulafki was fent, with a Body of Cavalry, againft a Party of the Enemy who had landed on Ogeechee River. He returned the next Day, having made a Number of Prifoners, and driven the Others on board their Veffels. On the 1ft of October, Colonel [John] White, of the Georgia Line, fucceeded, by an Extraordinary Stratagem, in capturing the Remainder of what was probably the fame Party, Veffels and all, as they had not dared to leave the River, through Fear of the French Fleet. White

were employed in landing and getting up the
Ordnance and Stores; a Work of Difficulty,
from the Want of proper Wheels to tranfport
them, the Cannon being on Ship Carriages.
On the Evening of the 23d, Ground was
broken; and on the 5th Inftant, the Batteries
of thirty-three Pieces of Cannon and nine Mortars were opened on the Enemy, and continued
with Intervals until the 8th, without the wifhed

had with him only Captain Etholm, three Soldiers, and his
Servant; but, knowing how much the Britifh were alarmed by
their Pofition, not being able to put to Sea, and having the
Army of the Allies between them and Savannah, he conceived
the Defign of frightening them into a Surrender. He kindled a
Number of Fires on the Shore, ranged in the Manner of a
Camp, rode about, giving Orders in fo loud a Voice as to be
heard on board the Veffels, and then, going out to the Enemy
with a Flag of Truce, fummoned them to furrender. Captain
French, of Delancey's Battalion, who commanded the Party,
believed that a large American Force was on Shore, and actually
furrendered his Detachment, and one hundred and thirty ftand
of Arms, the Crews of the Veffels, and the five Veffels themfelves, four of which were armed, the largeft mounting fourteen
Guns. Articles of Capitulation were drawn up and figned by
him. White pretended that it was difficult to reftrain the Ani-
mofity and the plundering Propenfity of his Men, and therefore
ordered the whole Band to go on Shore, without their Arms, and
follow three Guides, whom he would fend to them, by whom

for Effect. The Period having long since elapsed
which the Count had assigned for this Expedition, and the Engineers informing him that
much more Time must be spent, if he expected
to reduce the Garrison by regular Approaches,
and his longer Stay being impossible, Matters
were reduced to the Alternative of raising the
Siege immediately, and giving up all Thoughts
of Conquest, or attempting the Garrison by

they would be conducted to Lincoln's Army, while his Party
would follow in their Rear. They readily assented; for as most
of them were Tories, they had a great Dread of their Coun-
trymen who acted as Militia, since great Cruelties were often
practiced on the two Parties. White sent his three Soldiers to
guide them, and, remaining behind with Captain Etholm, collected a few Militia in the Neighborhood, with whom he overtook
his Prisoners, and brought them safely into Camp.

  "Colonel Lee gives this Story in his History of the War,
and adds: 'The Affair approaches too near the Marvellous to
have been admitted into these Memoirs, had it not been uniformly asserted, as uniformly accredited, and never contradicted.'
There is no Doubt of its Truth; as it is related in Lincoln's
private Manuscript Journal of the Siege, is mentioned in his
Letter to Congress, and, among his Papers, I have found Colonel
White's Letter to him, describing the Affair, and the original
Articles of Capitulation, signed by 'Thomas French, Captain
of De Lancey's First Battalion.' "—Bowen's *Life of Lincoln*, P.
305.

Affault.[1] The Latter was agreed on ; and on the Morning of the 9th the Attack was made ; and it proved unfuccefsful, and we were repulfed with fome Lofs. When the Count firft arrived, he informed us that he would remain on Shore eight Days only. He had fpent four Times that Number ; his Departure, therefore, became indifpenfable ; and to reëmbark his Ordnance and Stores claimed his next Attention. This was completed on the 10th. The fame Evening, having previoufly fent off our Sick, Wounded, and heavy Baggage, the American Troops left the Ground, reached Zubly's Ferry the next Morning, recroffed, and encamped that Night in Carolina.[2]

[1] "It was determined to make an Affault. This Meafure was forced on D'Eftaing by his marine Officers, who had remonftrated againft his continuing to rifk fo valuable a Fleet in its prefent unrepaired Condition on fuch a dangerous Coaft, in the hurricane Seafon, and at fo great a Diftance from the Shore that it might be furprifed by a Britifh Fleet. In a few Days the Lines of the Befiegers might have been carried into the Works of the Befieged ; but under thefe critical Circumftances no farther Delay could be admitted. To affault, or to raife the Siege was the only Alternative. Prudence would have dictated the Latter ; but a Senfe of Honor determined to adopt the Former." —Ramfay's *Hiftory of South Carolina,* i, 316.

[2] General Lincoln's Want of Succefs at Savannah, and fubfequent Defeat at Charlefton, did not abate the Confidence in

Engraved by T. Illman

MAJOR GENERAL

BENJAMIN LINCOLN,

The French Troops encamped, on the Night of the 10th, about two Miles from Savannah. They were, after twenty-four Hours, reëmbarked at Kincaid's Landing.

Our Difappointment is great; and what adds much to our Senfe of it, is the Lofs of a Number of brave Officers and Men, among them the late intrepid Count Pulafki.

Count D'Eftaing has undoubtedly the Intereft of America much at Heart. This he has evinced by coming to our Affiftance, by his conftant Attention during the Siege, his undertaking to reduce the Enemy by Affault, when he difpaired of effecting it otherwife, and by bravely putting himfelf at the Head of his

which he was held by the Commander-in Chief, by Congrefs, and by the People. He fubfequently participated in the Siege of Yorktown, was appointed Secretary of War, commanded the Troops fent againft Shay's Rebellion in Weftern Maffachufetts, and ferved on feveral important Commiffions. In 1788 he became Lieutenant-Governor of his native State. General Wafhington appointed him Collector of Bofton, and he lent his full Influence to the Meafures of the firft Prefident.

In 1806 he refigned his Office, under a Weight of growing Infirmities. He died at his Home in Hingham, Maff., May 9, 1810, at the Age of feventy-feven.—*Maff. Hift. Collections,* 2d Ser., iii, 233; Bowen's *Life of Lincoln;* Sparks's *Biog. Series,* xxiii.

Troops, and leading them to the Attack. In
our Service he has freely bled. I feel much for
him; for while he is fuffering the Diftrefs of
painful Wounds, he has to combat Chagrin. I
hope he will be confoled by the Affurance that,
although he has not fucceeded according to his
Wifhes and thofe of America, we regard with
high Approbation his Intentions to ferve us,
and that his Want of Succefs will not leffen
our Ideas of his Merits."

*Extract from the King's Speech to Parlia-
ment, November* 1, 1780.

* * * " BY the Force which the laft
Parliament put into my
Hands, and by the Bleffing of Divine Providence on the Bravery of my Fleets and Armies,
I have been enabled to withftand the formidable
Attempts of my Enemies, and to fruftrate the
great Expectations they had formed; and the
fignal Succeffes which have attended the Progrefs of my Arms in the Provinces of *Georgia*
and *Carolina*, gained with fo much Honour to
the Conduct and Courage of my Officers, and
to the Valour and Intrepidity of my Troops,

which have equalled their higheft Character in
any Age, will, I truft, have important Confe-
quences in bringing the War to a happy Con-
clufion: It is my moft earneft Defire to fee
this great End accomplifhed; but I am confi-
dent you will agree with me in Opinion, that
we can only fecure fafe and honourable Terms
of Peace by fuch powerful and refpectable Pre-
parations as fhall convince our Enemies that we
will not fubmit to receive the Law from any
Powers whatfoever; and that we are united to
a firm Refolution to decline no Difficulty or
Hazard in the Defence of our Country, and for
the Prefervation of our effential Interefts."

American Account of the Siege of Savannah.

Furnifhed by an Officer engaged in the Attack.[1]

" EARLY in Sept. 1779, the *Amazon* French
Frigate appeared off Charlefton Bar; the
Vifcompte de Fontanges, Adjutant General to
the Army under Count D'Eftaing, landed and
conferred with Gen. Lincoln, when an Attack
upon the Britifh Force in Savannah, by the

---

[1] Major Thomas Pinckney.

W

combined French Army, faid to confift of three thoufand Men, and one thoufand American Troops to be furnifhed by General Lincoln, was agreed upon. By Order of General Lincoln, Colonel Cambray of the Engineers, Captain Gadfden and myfelf, embarked on board the *Amazon*, then commanded by the celebrated Circumnavigator La Peroufe.[1] In a Day or two after we left Charlefton, we joined the French Fleet, confifting of twenty Ships of the Line, and feveral Frigates, when we went on board the *Languedoc*, to be under the immediate Command of Count D'Eftaing, who had defired that fome American Officers, acquainted with the French Language, might be fent to him. In paffing before Beaufort, D'Eftaing was apprifed that Colonel Maitland, with a confiderable Part of the Britifh Force, was ftationed at that Place, and was aware of the Advantages which would refult from preventing his Junction with the main Body at Savannah. Our Progrefs was

[1] After the Peace of 1783, he was appointed to conduct a fcientific Expedition on a Voyage of Difcovery. His laft Communication was dated February 7, 1788, from Botany Bay, and a Myftery hung over his Fate till 1827, when it was learned that his Ships were loft on one of the Iflands of the New Hebrides Group.

delayed fome Hours off the Bar; and it was
reported that fome of the fmaller Veffels were
preparing to enter, but the Plan was relinquifhed
becaufe the Pilots furnifhed from Charlefton
refufed to undertake to carry them in. This
was the firft great Error of this fhort, but difaftrous Campaign. The whole Britifh regular
Force amounted only to two thoufand five
hundred Men, of which Maitland commanded
eight hundred at Beaufort; had thefe been prevented from joining Prevoft at Savannah, it is
probable the Latter would have capitulated, or
certainly could not have made the fame formidable Refiftance. I know, however, from the
Acknowledgement of the principal Pilot, that
he did refufe to carry in the Veffels.

"The Fleet then proceeded off Savannah
Bar, where Information being received that the
Britifh had a Company of Regulars pofted on
Tybee Ifland, D'Eftaing determined to attack
them. Accordingly, he landed with the Officers
of his Staff, the three Americans, and his Body-
guard, compofed of a Subaltern's Command of
about twenty Marines; we marched near half
Mile in the Direction of the Fort, when D'Eftaing, looking back and feeing only his flender

Efcort, afked the Adjutant General, where were the Troops to reduce the Britifh Poft? M. de Fontanges anfwered that he had received no Directions to order any Troops for the Occafion. The General appeared much irritated, replying that he had informed him of the Object he had in View, and that it was his Duty to have brought with him the Number of Troops neceffary for the Occafion. While this was paffing, a Couple of Negroes came by, who being interrogated, informed that the Poft had been withdrawn early that Morning. This extraordinary Occurrence is mentioned to fhow fomething of the Manner of Proceeding of the Commander-in-chief of the Expedition, and of the Footing on which he ftood with the Officers under his Command.

"The Fleet then proceeded off Affeeba Sound, where about eighteen hundred Troops were embarked in the Boats of the Fleet, and proceeded at Night fall twelve Miles up the River to Beaulieu. The Order for landing, directed that the Boats fhould follow, as expeditioufly as they could, (in that in which the General embarked, a Lantern was hoifted,) and on reaching the Landing, the Troops were to range themfelves next to thofe whom they would find drawn up, without any Regard to Corps. It was fortunate for the General, whofe Boat being lighter than the Reft confiderably outrowed them, that a Britifh Poft with two Field-pieces had been withdrawn the preceding Day, or the Boats which arrived firft, muft have been greatly annoyed; the Bluff of Beaulieu commanding a long Reach of the River up which they paffed. The Landing with fuch a Body, would probably have been effected, but certainly not without confiderable Lofs. No Time was loft after the Landing of the Troops, in marching to Savannah; it appearing to be the Defire of the General to arrive there before the Day appointed for the Rendezvous with General Lincoln.

"The Morning after the Army encamped, within a fhort Diftance of Savannah, a Flag of Truce was fent in, requiring the Surrender of the Poft and Garrifon, to the *Army of His Moft Chriftian Majefty*. A Delay of twenty-four Hours for the Anfwer, was required and granted; before their Expiration, Maitland brought in his Detachment, and the Demand of Capitulation was rejected.

"General Lincoln, with the American Army, arrived near Savannah at the Time agreed upon, which was the 17th September, and on the 23d, the two Armies formed a Junction, and encamped together within about a Mile and a half of the Enemy's Lines, the French on the Right. Here I joined my Regiment, which being the Firſt of South Carolina, was encamped on the extreme Left of the Line.

"It appeared now to be the Determination of the Generals, to endeavour to carry the Poſt by regular Approaches; for the Enemy's Line of Defence, which was ſcarcely begun when D'Eſtaing's Summons was given, had, in that Interval of ten Days, become formidable; it extended along the ſandy Ridge or Bluff, on which Savannah is built, from the Swamp below the Town to Yamacraw Creek, which is its upper Boundary. It conſiſted of a Chain of Redoubts with Batteries, the whole covered in Front by a ſtrong Abbatis. The principal Battery appeared to be in the Centre of the Line, where ſtood, when we firſt approached it, a large public Building of Brick, but which diſappeared in one Night, and in a Day or two a formidable Battery was opened upon us from

its Site. The next Work in Importance was
the Spring Hill Redoubt, which was on their
extreme Right, and commanded Yamacraw
Creek, at the Mouth whereof was ftationed a
Britifh Galley. This Line was admirably
adapted to the Enemy's Force; if it had been
a clofed Line, their two thoufand five hundred
Troops could not have manned the Whole,
efpecially as they were obliged to have fome
flight Works on each Flank, and to pay fome
Attention to their Front on the River, as the
French had fent fome fmall Veffels of War with
a Bomb-ketch into the Back River, which is
only feparated from the main Channel by an
Ifland of Marfh. From the 23d September,[1]
when our Army firft broke Ground, we continued working in the Trenches with great
Affiduity. Our Batteries opened on the 5th of
October, but though well ferved, apparently
with little Effect. The Sap continued to be
pufhed forward until the 8th, when the Remon-
ftrance of the Officers of the French Fleet
againft their being detained longer on the Coaft,
induced Count D'Eftaing to inform General

---

[1] I kept no Memorandum of the Dates, but have referred to
Gen. Moultrie's Memoirs for them.

Lincoln that he muſt withdraw his Force; but
to prove his Deſire to ſerve the Cauſe, he offered to coöperate in an Aſſault upon the
Britiſh Lines. This appears to have been accepted as the *Piſaller*, and on that Day we were
ordered to parade near the Left of the Line at
1 o'clock of the next Morning, where we were
to be joined by the French, and to march to
the Attack in the following Order:—The
French Troops were to be divided into three
Columns, the Americans into two, the Heads
of which were to be poſted in a Line, with
proper Intervals at the Edge of the Wood
adjoining the open Space of five or ſix hundred
Yards between it and the Enemy's Line, and at
4 o'clock in the Morning, a little before Daylight, the whole was, on a Signal being given,
to ruſh forward and attack the Redoubts and
Batteries oppoſed to their Front. The American Column of the Right, which adjoined the
French, were to be preceded by Pulaſki, with
his Cavalry and the Cavalry of South Carolina,
and were to follow the French until they approach the Edge of the Wood, when they were
to break off and take their Poſition. This
Column was compoſed of the Light Infantry

under Col. Laurens, of the 2d Regiment of South Carolina, and the 1ſt Battalion of Charleſton Militia. The ſecond American Column conſiſted of the 1ſt and 5th South Carolina Regiments, commanded by Brigadier General M'Intoſh of Georgia. A Corps of French Weſt India Troops, under the Viſcompte de Noailles, the Artillery, and ſome American Militia, formed the Reſerve under General Lincoln.

" A faint Attack by the South Carolina Militia and Georgians, under Brigadier General Huger, was ordered to be made on the Enemy's Left; but, inſtead of the French Troops being paraded ſo as to march off at 4 o'clock, it was near four before the Head of that Column reached our Front. The whole Army then marched towards the Skirt of the Wood in one long Column, and as they approached, the opèn Space were to break off into the different Columns, as ordered for the Attack. But, by the Time the firſt French Column had arrived at the open Space, the Day had fairly broke, when Count D'Eſtaing, without waiting until the other Columns had arrived at their Poſition, placed himſelf at the Head of his firſt Column,

X

and rufhed forward to the Attack. But this
Body was fo feverely galled by the Grape-fhot
from the Batteries as they advanced, and by
both Grape-fhot and Mufketry when they
reached the Abbatis, that, in fpite of the Effort
of the Officers, the Column got into Confufion
and broke away to their Left toward the Wood
in that Direction ; the fecond and the third
French Columns fhared fucceffively the fame
Fate, having the additional Difcouragement of
feeing as they marched to the Attack, the Repulfe and Lofs of their Comrades who had
preceded them. Count Pulafki, who, with the
Cavalry, preceded the right Column of the
Americans, proceeded gallantly until ftopped
by the Abbatis, and before he could force
through it, received his mortal Wound. In
the mean Time, Colonel Laurens at the Head
of the Light Infantry, followed by the 2d South
Carolina Regiment, and 1ft Battalion Charlefton
Militia, attacked the Spring Hill Redoubt, got
into the Ditch and planted the Colours of the
2d Regiment on the Berm, but the Parapet was
too high for them to fcale it under fo heavy a
Fire, and after much Slaughter they were driven
out of the Ditch. When General Pulafki was

about to be removed from the Field, Colonel
D. Horry, to whom the Command of the Cavalry devolved, afked what were his Directions.
He anfwered, 'follow my Lancers to whom I
have given my order of Attack.' But the Lancers were fo feverely galled by the Enemy's
Fire, that they alfo inclined off to the Left,
and were followed by all the Cavalry, breaking
through the American Column, who were attacking the Spring Hill Redoubt. By this
Time the 2d American Column headed by Gen.
M'Intofh, to which I was attached, arrived at
the Foot of the Spring Hill Redoubt, and fuch
a Scene of Confufion as there appeared is not
often equalled. Col. Laurens had been feparated from that Part of his Command that had
not entered the Spring Hill Ditch by the
Cavalry, who had borne it before them into the
Swamp to the Left, and when we marched up,
inquired *if we had feen them.* Count D'Eftaing
was wounded in the Arm, and endeavouring to
rally his Men, a few of whom with a Drummer
he had collected. General M'Intofh did not
fpeak French, but defired me to inform the Commander-in-chief that his Column was frefh, and
that he wifhed his Directions, where, under

prefent Circumftances, he fhould make the Attack. The Count ordered that we fhould move
more to the Left, and by no Means to interfere
with the Troops he was endeavouring to rally;
in purfuing this Direction we were thrown too
much to the Left, and before we could reach
Spring Hill Redoubt, we had to pafs through
Yamacraw Swamp, then wet and boggy, with
the Galley at the Mouth annoying our left Flank
with Grape-fhot. While ftruggling through
this Morafs, the firing flacked, and it was reported that the whole Army had retired. I was
fent by General M'Intofh to look out from the
Spring Hill, where I found not an Affailant
ftanding. On reporting this to the General, he
ordered a Retreat, which was effected without
much Lofs, notwithftanding the heavy Fire of
Grape-fhot with which we were followed.

"The Lofs of both Armies in killed and
wounded amounted to 637 French and 457
Americans,[1] 1000.[2] The Irifh Brigade in the
French Service, and our 2d Regiment, particularly diftinguifhed themfelves and fuffered moft.
The Lofs of the Britifh amounted only to fifty-
five.

[1] Moultrie.   [2] Marfhall.

" Thus was this fine Body of Troops facri-
ficed by the Imprudence of the French General,
who, being of fuperior Grade, commanded the
Whole. If the French Troops had left their
Encampment in Time for the different Corps
to have reached their Pofitions, and the Whole
attacked together, the Profpect of Succefs would
have been infinitely better, though even then it
would have been very doubtful on Account of
the Strength of the Enemy's Line, which was
well fupplied by Artillery. But if Count D'Eftaing had reflected a Moment, he muft have
known, that attacking with a fingle Column
before the Reft of the Army could have reached
their Pofition, was expofing the Army to be
beaten in Detail. In fact the Enemy, who were
to be affailed at once on a confiderable Part of
their Front, finding themfelves only attacked at
one Point, very deliberately concentrated their
whole Fire on the affailing Column, and that
was repeated as faft as the different Corps were
brought up to the Attack. General Lincoln
had the Command of the Referve and covered
the Retreat ; if he had led the Attack, I think
the Event could not have been fo difaftrous,
and I am warranted in this Opinion by the At-

tack he made on the Enemy's Lines at Stono, where, when he found how ftrongly the Enemy were entrenched, although his Light Infantry, on both Flanks, had gained fome Advantage, withdrew the Troops without any confiderable Lofs.

" The Similarity in the Refult of this Attack on Savannah, and that of the Britifh on New Orleans in 1815, is remarkable; the Loffes of the Affailants and their Enemies was nearly in equal Proportion. Neither can Packenham efcape the Cenfure of Precipitation, in urging the Attack when he knew the fcaling Ladders he had ordered were not brought up, and before Colonel Thornton had got Poffeffion of our Batteries on the Weft Side of the River, which, if brought to bear on the right Flank of the American Line, muft have made an important Diverfion in Favour of his Attack."—Garden's *Anecdotes of the American Revolution,* Brooklyn Ed., 1865, iii, 19.

*French Account of D'Eftaing's Attempt
upon Savannah in Georgia.*

[From the Paris Gazette of Jan. 7, 1780.]

*Summary of the Operations of the King's Squadron
commanded by the Count D'Eftaing, Vice Admiral
of France, after the taking of Grenada, and the
Naval Engagement off that Ifland with Byron's
Squadron.*

A DETACHMENT of the King's Ships
and Frigates, under the Orders of Captain de Suffren, went to make the Iflands of
Curiacou and Union Capitulate, and received
the Oath of Allegiance of the Inhabitants.
The Sieur Montet, Governor of the Ifland of
St. Vincent, performed the fame Operation in
the Iflands of Becouya; the Surrender of the
other little Grenadines followed immediately
that of the principal Iflands.

The 22d of July, the King's Squadron appeared before St. Chriftopher's, where the Englifh Squadron was at Anchor under the Batteries
in the Road. The Englifh Admiral did not
think proper to accept the Battle.

After remaining two Days before St. Chriftopher's, the King's Squadron failed for St.

Domingo with the trading Fleet of the French Windward Iflands. The Count D'Eftaing difpatched all thefe Ships to Europe, which were joined by thofe of the Leeward Iflands, under the Protection of the Ships *le Protecteur* and *la Fier*, and the Frigates *la Minerve* and *l'Alemene*.

With the Remainder of his Squadron he fteered for the Coafts of the Continent of America. A Gale of Wind he met with the 2d of September, whilft at Anchor before the Mouth of Savannah, prevented his going up more Northward. Moft of his Ships were difabled, and five of them had their Rudders broken.

The Repair of the King's Ships required a confiderable Time in a Country where naval Stores are hard to be come at. That Circumftance decided the Count d'Eftaing to undertake the Siege of Savannah with the Troops he had on board his Ships, which were joined by 2,000 Men from the United States of North America, under the Command of General Lincoln.

The French Troops confifted of 2,823 Europeans, draughted from the Regiments of Armagnac, Champagne, Auxerrois, Agenois, Garinois, Cambrefis, Haynault, Foix, Dillon, Walfh, le Cap, la Gaudeloupe, la Martinique

and Port au Prince, including a Detachment of
the Royal Corps of Infantry of the Marine,
the Volunteers of Vallelle, the Dragoons, and
156 Volunteer Grenadiers, lately raifed at Cape
François. The coloured Troops confifted of
545 Volunteer Chaffeurs, Mulattoes and Negroes, newly raifed at St. Domingo.

The Total of the Troops of the Befiegers,
including the 2,000 Americans, amounted to
5,524 Men.

The Englifh had in Savannah 3,055 Englifh
European Troops, 80 Cherokee Savages, and
4,000 Negroes. The Total of the Troops of
the Befieged was 7,165 Men, under the Command of General Prevoft.

The 15th of September the Englifh General
was fummoned to furrender the Place, and on
his Refufal the Siege was begun. It was carried
on with as much Vigour as the fmall Number
of Workmen would admit of. The Enemy
made a Sally the 24th of September, and were
repulfed with Lofs, and the Sieur O'Dun pur-
fued them as far as their Intrenchments. The
Impoffibility of continuing a Siege in Form
againft fuperior Forces, decided the Count
d'Eftaing to order the Attack on the Entrench-
ments the 9th of October. The Enemy, being

Y

informed by Deferters of the Plan of the Attack, had prepared their Defence on the Side intended to be furprifed.

The French and American Troops attacked with the greateft Vigour, and returned three Times to the Charge; but the Superiority of Numbers forced them to give Way.

The Seafon was too far advanced for the Count d'Eftaing to hope he could terminate the Operations of a Siege; he was afraid left one of thofe Gales, fo frequent on the Coaft of Georgia, fhould drive his Ships out of the Road, and oblige him to put to Sea, in Order to fave them, and thus abandon the Troops employed in the Expedition. He refolved to raife the Siege. The Retreat was made in the beft Order, and without being molefted.

The King's Troops reëmbarked the 20th of October; only two Days after the Rudders of the Ships could be repaired and placed.

The greateft Union has fubfifted between the combined Forces.

The Count de Dillon, the Vifcount de Noailles, the Marquis de Pont de Naux, the Baron de Steding, the Vifcount de Fontages, Colonel and the Sieur O'Dun, Lieutenant Colonel, particularly diftinguifhed themfelves in an Operation, as painful by the Fatigues of a Ser vice rendered continual by the fmall Number of Men, as it was glorious for them, by the Dangers to which they were perpetually expofed, and by the different Manœuvres with which they were charged.

The Chevalier de Trolong du Romain, and the Count de Chaftenet de Puyfegur, have proved, by conducting the King's Lighter *la Truite*, under the very Batteries of the Town of Savannah, that an armed Sloop, laden with Artillery of the Calibre of 12, too ftrong for its Pattern, could back itfelf againft land Batteries of the largeft Calibre.

Total of the Killed, 15 Officers, and 168 Subalterns and Soldiers.

Total of the Wounded, 43 Officers, and 411 Subalterns and Soldiers.—*New Jerfey Journal*, ii, lxxi, June 21, 1780.

Count Pulaſki.

AMONG the Loffes of the Allies before Savannah, none was more feverely felt than that of Count Cafimir Pulafki. Defcended from a noble Houfe in Poland, and reared in the Love of Liberty, he had long contended againft the Tyranny that was crufhing his native Country; and when Refiftance was no longer of avail, he fled to Turkey in the Hope of continuing the Conteft againft Ruffia, but a Peace in 1774 put an End to this, and he came to offer his Services to America.

His active and ardent martial Spirit commended him to the Favor of Wafhington; and, having ferved. without Rank as a Volunteer with much Succefs at the Battle of Brandywine, was appointed by Congrefs, September 5th, 1777, to the Command of a Troop of Horfe, with the Rank of Brigadier. In 1778 he was authorized to raife an independent Corps, compofed of three Companies of Cavalry and three of Foot, which received the Name of " Pulafki's Legion." While this was being organized, he was ftationed at Bethlehem, Pa.; and the Protection he afforded to the Female Members of the Moravian Community at that Place was rewarded by the Prefentation of a beautiful Silk Banner, taftefully embroidered; and which, after being faved at the Battle of Savannah, was brought North, and finally was depofited with the Maryland Hiftorical Society.

Conflicting Accounts have come down to us relating to the Place of General Pulaſki's Place of Burial; and when the noble Monument to his Memory was erected at Savannah, a metallic Caſe, holding what were ſuppoſed to be his mortal Remains, was placed within the Plinth, alongſide of the Corner Stone. The Weight of Evidence, however, decides in the Belief, that he died on Board the *Waſp*, and was buried under Water, on the Return of the Army to Charleſton. The Subject is fully ſtated in Prof. Stevens's *Hiſtory of Georgia*, from which Work this Notice is abridged.

Upon the Viſit of the Marquis de La Fayette to Savannah, in 1825, the Corner Stone was laid for a Monument to Count Pulaſki, on Chippeway Square, and another to General Greene on Pulaſki Square.

An Attempt was made to raiſe the Funds for this Object, but failed, as did alſo an Effort to combine the two Enterpriſes in a "Greene and Pulaſki Monument," although a conſiderable Sum was raiſed by Lottery for this Purpoſe. On the 11th of October, 1853, the Corner Stone of another Monument to Pulaſki was laid, and the Structure was finiſhed at about the Beginning of the late Rebellion.

An Engraving, reprefenting the Pulafki Monument, and a full Defcription, and Account of laying the Corner Stone, are given in White's *Hiftory of Georgia*, P. 308.

INDEX.

Z